Who Fishing Was Serious?

by

Ed Rychkun

ISBN 978-1-927066-08-9

Editing: Hope Rychkun
Cover: by Ed Rychkun

THE CONTENTS OF THIS BOOK

FOREWORD

Have you ever sat and thought about those many fishing situations that were so funny that you really had a tough time containing yourself? You know the ones... those that seem to come out after you've had a few drinks and the group starts frothing with the fish tales. I mean the "roll on the floor" ones that make your six-pack... the one under your belly fat... hurt. I have always found the funniest ones were when someone goes through elaborate re-search to find the sure-kill scientific method to catch those small-brained fish and gets skunked. Can you think back to those many times where you heard someone telling you all his secrets and you watched each secret fail? Then there are the situations that come about when a strange sequence of calamities unfolds when some poor victim just appears to have unusual bad luck.

At the heart of this, it is pretty obvious that most anglers take fishing serious. Otherwise, why would anyone spend so much money on catching that scrawny fish? Or what would possess someone to go out so early, brave the weather, fight insects, or punish themselves getting to the perfect fishing hole? This has to be a serious sport, particularly if you compared the cost per pound of that fish against the same one in the local fishing market!

But no, it is all for fun! It is not serious at all. It is all about spending money, getting skunked, frozen, or punished. Anyway, the cooler of beer, the great outdoors, the great buddies, and that big strike far outweigh those other discomforts, don't they? Why of course they do!

I have always found the most humorous escapades were those that pitted technology and supposed know-how against that primitive creature called a fish. What always gave me a chuckle was when someone, who had all those new devices and determination, ends up being skunked. Or better still, when it was not science but pure luck that made the day. Now this book is not intended to belittle the art of angling, nor is it intended to make a mockery of the technical attack at fishing, but let's get serious. Can we really be serious about this sport? There is certainly much humour in its application because so many times, the best of tactics and techniques fall victim to the peculiar odds of failure. There are many other situations that are just unbelievably funny after they happen and you just have to shake your head in bewilderment as to how such a sequence of calamities could possibly happen so fast. The best, of course, are when no one gets hurt.

I have to say that I have had my share of these. I found endless humour in that contrast that occurs between a supposed expert and that dumb fish. My brother, Mike, and myself always showed the greatest contrast. Mike was a very analytical engineer. He was so analytical and precise by nature that you really wondered why he ever took to the art of fishing. He found his fun in going to great lengths to rationalize techniques and plan his next attack. He was so serious about this. But best of all, he had a sense of humour and could actually laugh at his failures, when his superior analytical ability was thwarted and these fish that always seemed to elude his technology. Of course, I was just the opposite in that I was there for the fun of it. The craziest situations were, however, when he fell victim to those calamities. I was always amazed at the persistence, his wry humour, his constant grin and his dedication to enjoying it regardless of outcome. I loved that guy – like a brother they say – but it would have been hard for anyone to read that because we were so opposite.

So I decided to publish this book because I found these situations so funny. I have to dedicate this book to him sadly he had to leave the planet early but he will always be remembered and his antics are enshrined here. When I put the stories on paper and read them now, years later, they seemed even funnier. I was indeed influenced by my older brother's insatiable desire to treat fishing so serious. I have to admit that it very rarely ended up that way because most often, something funny happened. That's why I called this book **"Who Said Fishing Was Serious?"** Is it? You decide.

Enjoy it.

Ed Rychkun

MIKEY CATCHES HIM(SELF) A GIANT FISH

The scene opens on a Friday evening as we sit around snorting back a few beer during a poker game and discussing the politics of the day. There is something bothering Mike as he fidgets and ignores the conversation. "Hey Mike," I asked, "what's bugging you, you don't seem to be too interested in current events?"

"You're absolutely right, I was at the Army & Navy yesterday picking up some new hot lures and got into a conversation with a guy who said he was a world expert. He told me that this 3-ounce lure he was selling was a sure fire bet on those Coho running up the Harrison River. He said they are so bloody thick down under the old rail bridge that you can actually snag them! So I picked these five killer lures... look at the fantastic colours!"

It was pretty hard to contain ourselves. We all rolled our eyes in unison. Here we go again with one of Mike's new ideas. The colours were dazzling, red and blue stripes with gold fleck, oddly contorted to look like a fish. The lure was immense. The three-barbed hook at the end looked more like it had been cut off a gaff. "Did you get some logging cable to haul this thing, Mike," I snorted, "or are you planning to knock the fish out with it?" Les couldn't contain himself. "Mike, we could use that thing for a boat anchor, I hope it doesn't fall out of the car hooked up or we will pull the ass-end out of the car…" We all snorted as Mike leered.

"Mike, I've seen it all, what horseshit you tell," said Les after he contained himself, "I can't count the number of times you got sucked in by some so called expert but I will certainly verify that I heard the Coho were at the mouth of the river. I am amazed that you would buy these things… have you ever heard that Coho prefer eggs?"

Mike was determined to stick to his new information. "Look, you guys can laugh all you like but I'm heading out first thing so if you want to come, you better be ready. Here I am offering to share these with you and all I get is this?" What could we say? The fact was the Coho were running so we agreed to go.

So it's Saturday morning, 6:00 AM at Mom's home in Mission. Mike is already out packing up the biggest rod he has. It was all rigged up, ready to go. Now this rod is a 15-foot beauty, with a handle on it like a log. The spinning reel on it was the size of an oilcan. "Jeez, Mike, how the hell are you proposing to carry that in the car? We will need to strap that thing on the roof to get it there... don't you think it's overkill?" "Look, Ed, I will take my car and I will get this thing inside. All I have to do is unzip the back window out of my convertible and stick it out. You are the guys that are going to look stupid when that 12 pound Coho hits that lure!"

It's now time to get serious and off we go, the three of us with this massive pole sticking out the back. Mike refused to take it apart since he always liked to get right to the hole without wasting time. The fact was that this was his tactic to get to the best spot first. Kilby Park was about an hour away, a nice quiet place close to the river. Mike was out of the car like a shot. He had cleverly rigged his gear back at the house so he could get the jump on us. He knew exactly where he was going to cast that killer lure and he wanted no one to take his spot. Les and I casually grabbed the cooler and our gear and headed towards the railway bridge. The water looked cool and clear... "Dammit," said Les, "this is perfect, we may even catch a Coho... snap me a cool one and pass me some roe Ed, I am feeling lucky."

As we approached the bank, Mike was already there, getting ready for one of his expert casts. "See that deep dark swirl over there by the bridge pylon?" Mike reported, "That's where this baby is headed... did you guys bring the net with you?" Les and I just looked at each other and rolled our eyes in unison. An amazing sequence of events was about to unfold. Mike lifted his monster pole to 1:00 o'clock, turned his head slightly to make sure we were watching the show, and then swatted the rod down with one helluva swat. Somehow, Mike had positioned the giant lure low down behind him and had forgot to flip the guide back on his reel. When he executed the swat forward with the rod, the line started to move at about the vertical position so the lure came straight up to hook him right on the arse. The swat was so fierce that it almost lifted his arse up six inches as that massive barbed hook embedded itself into the delicate meat of the right cheek of his gluteus maximus. There was dead silence as Mike waited for that instant when the lure sailed elegantly to its destination. Suddenly he felt that incredible pain. The only thing that saved Mike from tearing a chunk of his butt off was the fact his swat wasn't any longer, but it was sufficient to embed the hook deeply into the muscle.

Well, Les and I actually broke up and lost it. We looked at each other for a flash second before we started to roar with laughter. Mike just stood there, frozen. It was an infectious process... the harder Les laughed, the more I laughed... in fits that just got more intense. And the fact that Mike just stood there dumbfounded with his line hanging from his pants just made it worse. After a few minutes, when the tears from our eyes cleared, you could see Mike reaching back in slow motion to gently probe the damage. As we got up and approached him, you could see shock in his eyes. This hook was so well embedded that it was not possible to touch it without causing severe pain. Well, this is where you really find out who your buddies are... when you're in deep doodoo like Mike was. He was in severe pain. He couldn't move, as the hook was too deep. His pants were bloody from the wound and there was no way to sever it as his pants were permanently stuck by the embedded hook.

Although the poor guy was in agony, it was difficult for Les and I to contain ourselves. We knew deep down Mike's ego was suffering the most and that he was actually OK... he probably couldn't bleed to death in an hour. If anyone had seen this, it would have been an incredibly funny sight as we helped Mike walk stiff-legged to his car with a snipped line and lure hanging on his trousers. It was even funnier getting him in and driving an hour back to the house. It was one of the only times that Mike was very, very quiet. But the funniest part of all was watching Mom cutting Mike's special $50 fishing pants away from his body with the scissors, and then using a razor blade to cut that massive hook out of his right cheek. "Yep," Les used to say, "Mike sure caught a big one that day." But I would always think back on that day and wonder *how could anyone treat fishing as a serious matter*...

NEVER UNDER ESTIMATE THE TECHNOLOGY OF A SIMPLE NET

I t was the first morning of our fishing trip. The sky was clear, the birds were chirping and the lake was as smooth as a mirror. The smell of bacon in the camp air gave the morning the final crown. Mike was rummaging through his new flatfish box. It was time to test our skills again to bring back some fish for the new smoker. It was now 7:00 AM and you could hear the purr of outboards on the lake. Mike was becoming impatient. He couldn't stand it any longer..."Ed, we've got to get out there, I can feel the big ones biting. I know exactly where they are this time... I have a hot feeling about this silver and black flatfish and just look at the water. I can see risers everywhere." Grabbing the rod and the tackle box, I downed my coffee and said: "All right let's go I can't stand the harassment any longer."

Bleary eyed and thick headed from all the wine last night; I begrudgingly headed to the boat. We were on the lake at 7:15 AM. I was waiting for the next lecture on where we would find the biggest fish in the lake. Mike started his froth. "Ok Ed, this flatfish is hot but since I am not sure about the colour, why don't you try an orange one. Since it's early morning, I think the fish may be down about 20 feet, so I am going to troll with 2 small weights and let out 50 pulls. Why don't you go for 50 pulls and 1 weight Ed. The sun is still behind that mountain and the water looks fairly deep along that side, so let's troll along that shoreline."

I really couldn't have cared less. We trolled for about 20 minutes and there was no action. Mike said "I'm going down deeper with 3 weights and 10 more pulls but I am going to change to a blue and red, then head towards that bay over there." After 15 more minutes, and no action, I said "Mike, give me a break, you really don't have a clue where these fish are, do you?"

But by now I was waking up. I was stuck out there listening to this madman, but I had decided to go with the flow. Mike was still keen. "Well, I think we should take a sweep around the bay one more time. There is no action at these depths on this flatfish, so I am going back up to fish on top with a Spratley." After

50 pulls and 5 minutes, I felt a nibble on the line. "Mike, I just had a nibbler back there, I think we should take another sweep over that area and you should come back up close to surface with your flatfish." "Ok, I'll go for 1 weight and 60 pulls." About 3 minutes into the sweep over the same area Mike's rod showed a quick jerk, followed by a silver flash about 75 feet back as the trout rose to surface trying to spit the plug. "Faaantaaastic," Mike shouted, "what a beauty! Get your eyeballs on that monster..." It was indeed a spectacle of trout aerobatics that that 20 inch trout per-formed.

This fish tried everything. He had to be the biggest, strongest rainbow in the little lake. First he headed out to cross my line. He dove under and headed towards the other side of the boat. Mike looked like he was doing aero-bics to Jane Fonda, juggling his rod over and twisting back and forth to each side as the trout struggled against Mike's mighty rod. I just watched in amazement, as things just seemed funnier and funnier at Mike's end of the boat.

Mike was in a state. His end of the boat looked like a tornado hit it. His fishing box was turned over, plugs all over the bottom. His coffee had fallen over the side and he had tangled the boat's line around his feet. It was indeed a spectacle to watch. It was also difficult to contain myself, wishing I had brought the video. But in all fairness, I choked back my laughter and tried to be serious. "Congratulations Mike, I've got to admit it... you obviously got the hot item for the day... blue and red flatfish, 60 pulls and 1 weight, right?" There was only dead silence. I could see that Mike was scanning the boat for a net. There was some anguish on his face. The sight was getting to be too much for me. My line was tangled. He was frozen, tangled in gear and ropes, holding his rod outwards trying to keep this monster from plunging under the motor, and I was snorting at the other end of the boat. Finally Mike blew.

"Why you dumb shit, why don't you smarten up and net this bloody thing, Ed?" As we looked at each other, there was that silly feeling that the other guy was the one that was supposed to bring it. "Didn't you bring it?" I squeaked, "It was beside your fishing gear." Well, the rest was predictable.

The picture of disappointment was a strange contrast to the picture of confusion at the end of the boat. Mike knew he was on his own and this fish was mightier than the 6-pound test line. As he brought the monster close to the boat he readied himself for the pull that would hopefully bring it aboard. No such luck. The trout had one last spurt and broke away. First there was dead silence. Then we looked at each other and started to laugh. The roar of laughter that followed could be heard to the end of the lake. It was a contrast that I will not forget. ***How could I ever take fishing serious after that***?

UNCLE BILL'S
SPECIAL BLASTERS

U ncle Bill was an unusual fellow. He was one of those very resourceful fellows with a Ukrainian background. He grew up in the prairies so they had to be resourceful. When he came to BC in the 60's, he ended up buying an unusual property on a lake on Vancouver Island. Uncle Bill was a true old-fashioned guy and liked to feed his family on game that he would hunt or fish, then freeze. At that time, there was, of course, less people and more game to get so Bill was pretty faithful to his responsibility.

Bill was exceptionally resourceful when it came to getting game, especially fish and he was always resourceful when it came to finding ways to get them. He was always trying out the latest gizmo. I'd say Bill was a border case between someone who was a real inventing genius and a true nutcase. My brother used to hang around with him a lot while he was going to University so I think that is where he picked up a lot of traits to tenaciously pit technology against nature. Uncle Bill was a fantastic teacher, always sharing his inventions. If there were a new gizmo, Bill would build one of his own with new enhanced modifications. And he never isolated this stuff to fishing or hunting. If there was some way to improve his daily life, whether it was the car, the truck, machinery, tools, you name it, Bill was there building a new contraption and looking to patent it for a fortune.

So Bill was a pretty unusual guy. He was always full of fun as well so as a kid it was a really special event to visit him. After a few shots of vodka, Bill could keep everyone spellbound with his weird humour, his new gizmos and his stories. Bill's house was also a pretty unusual place. It was an old shack built on a big dock. He said it was pretty cool because he didn't have to pay any taxes on it as it was not a houseboat and it was not on land. The old house was on stilts and connected to the dock that had some outbuildings on it. After a few years, Bill had created a fairly monolithic structure here. He just added poles and stilts and shacks to his hearts content. It was pretty cool and very convenient as he could tie up his 14-foot aluminium boat and fish anytime. And as he was close to a lot of bush, hunting was pretty good too.

One weekend, we went out to visit him. It was an all day excursion because you had to take the ferry across to Nanaimo. He was of course thrilled to see us and insisted that we stay the weekend so he could show us some great things he had discovered. Mike was always impressed with his uncle. He and his wife were extremely hospitable, full of fun and of course we would stay. Bill immediately got some home brew out that he said was a new recipe with some extra kick in it. Of course the Ukrainian garlic sausage and dill pickles were essential. The sausage was his own special recipe made from venison and the pickles were a special recipe he brought from the prairies that he had modified a bit with some hot peppers.

"You boys will love this stuff." He said, "This lean meat will absorb the booze and keep you from getting drunk. The pickles are special. I call 'em fiery Bill's pickles and they are sure to light your toilet paper in the morning!" As we downed the first shot glass and chased it with the sausage, I could see why you needed the sausage. "Man alive, Bill," I choked, "this stuff has the kick of a mule!" Bill just guffawed. "I told you Eddy, it's very powerful triple distilled moonshine, but here, the second shot goes down much easier."

Well, the bullshit ran thick that afternoon. It was hard to tell with Bill what was real and what was not but the way he told the stories was always so credible. We each took a roll of sausage, Bill took the moonshine and he took us on a tour of the place. I was absolutely amazed at the contraptions and devices that Bill had created in this labyrinth of shacks. It seemed that every one of these was being patented and would get him a fortune... sooner or later. By 7:00PM it was getting dark and I could hear the generator kick in to high gear as the house lights turned on. "Boys, that's my new invention. It has a special sensor that starts the extra capacity when it reaches a threshold. That way I can use a small system when low power is utilized and save fuel." I just shook my head.

It was Mike who started the next series of conversations on fishing. "Bill," he said, "what's hot for catching trout in this lake?"

"Mike, I will tell you the best goddam thing is the willow leaf. I use three of them behind the boat. I have added some special designed flashers that send out vibrations to these fish. I think I invented one that makes them horny and they strike at anything behind the line. I am just trying to get a patent on this flasher. They're also good for scaring the crows out of the garden so they have dual function and I think I can make a fortune with this one." "How do you have three leafs behind the boat?" Mike asked, "They must get tangled."

"No way, Mike," Bill chuckled, "wait till you see my new contraption. I put two booms on my cartop boat and I have a pulley system that drops a ten-pound lead ball down to 30 feet. I then have a clip that holds the tackle down there and releases the line when the fish bite. There is another clip at the top of the boom. I think I can make a fortune on this thing! That way I can swing two lines out and fish deep and have the other directly behind me close to surface. Smart, hey?"

I had to admit, it was pretty cool. Mike was really impressed.

"But let me tell you guys, that's a tough way to fish. I am a meat fisherman and I go for getting them fast so those things are for you fellows that have lots of time and don't have

23

to feed the family." Mike led into it. "So what's your special invention here?" he asked.

"Look boys, I will let you in on a special method that works in the dark. I can get us a couple dozen in one shot." Well that was Mike's cue. "Holy shit, Bill, a method that works in the dark and gets lots of fish! Can you show us tonight?"

"Sure thing boys," Bill beamed. "We will need to boil some eggs first and we will need a big net and a flashlight. Maybe there are some boiled eggs in the, fridge already. Hey Martha" he yelled, "are there any boiled eggs?"

"Yes, Bill, if you haven't eaten them with that sausage yet." she replied.

I couldn't figure this one out. It really had me mystified as to what the hell he was up to. "OK boys, you peel six eggs and bring the moonshine out on the dock. I will get the flashlight, net and other stuff and meet you there."

"Jeez, Ed," Mike said, "this is really going to be interesting. I can't figure out what the old bugger is going to do. I never thought fish would go for eggs at night, did you?" We were

getting pretty pissed by now and it was difficult to peel the eggs. It was even more
difficult to get down the steps onto the dock
without falling in the water, as the lighting was
not that great. We got to the end of the dock
where we could barely see Bill. He took a look
at the eggs and said. "Hey you dummies, I
need the shells, not the eggs. You can leave
these as they go good with the moonshine.
Mike and I looked at each other and said nothing. He went up to get the shells. You could
hear him stumble down to the dock.

Bill took the eggshells and he told Mike to
crush them into small particles, and then put
them back in the pot for the next step. He
then told me to shine the flashlight for him
while he geared up, as he called it. Mike
couldn't stand it. "Bill, for Christ sake, what
are you going to do?" Bill was pretty cool
about it. "Well, boys, pay attention. I have
water proof baggies here with a rock in it.
Over here I have a six inch waterproof blasting
fuse and a blasting cap that I put on the end
of the fuse and crimp…" "Shit, I know what
that is," Mike interrupted, "that's what we
used for blasting stumps out on the farm. We
would use the fuse to give time to blow the
cap and the cap, inserted into the dynamite,
would blow the stump out of the ground…."

"That's right, Mike, except we are not using the dynamite. But maybe that's a good idea if we find a school of fish tomorrow with my new fish finder. Now, when I ignite the fuse, I gives it about five 5 seconds before the cap explodes. With the rock in the bag, it will get down about 20 feet by then, then it blows. This will send a shock wave through the water that gets amplified by the density of water and stuns the fish. They just float up to the surface and we can net them. I am going to put two down tonight so you boys can take some fish home for your Mom tomorrow."

"Shit, Bill, that's absolutely ingenious. What a smart bugger you are, but what gets the fish over here?" Bill beamed, "Well, that's what the egg shells are for. Before I drop the Bill Blasters, I call them; you drop the egg shells shining the flashlight down over them as they fall. As they fall slowly, they shimmer and vibrate like spoons, attracting the fish to this area. These look like a school of minnows to them. I then drop the blaster and then you will hear a WHOOOOMP as the shock wave stuns them. They will just float to the top and we net them."

This was cool. The wind had picked up a bit. Now the event was on. Bill gave the instructions. "OK, Mike, egg shells in. Make sure you keep the light on them as you drop them at the end of the dock. Try to make a steady stream. I want you to do it in two batches. The first batch will get them coming over and the second is when I will give them the blaster." As Mike dropped the first batch, I could see them glitter downward as they fell. Bill waited for the second batch, lit the first fuse and dropped it on the left side of the dock. He quickly went over to the other side and dropped blaster number 2. "Get ready boys, here she blows!"

The next sequence should go down in history. It took exactly twenty seconds. I still recall every part of the sequence in awe. Bill dropped the first bag but the tie was not done up well... too much moonshine I guess. The rock dropped out and went down, the bag with the explosive caught a wind gust and drifted back against the outboard motor and hung by the gas hose. The first blast ignited the hose and set the gas tank on fire. Mike got such a start; he fell off the dock into the water with the flashlight and the bottle of moonshine. As he hit the water, the second blast let go with a loud WHOOOOMP! Then the gas tank exploded. Fortunately it was a small one but it was enough to break the main support beam for the outside shithouse that had its porta tank suspended above the dock. Somehow, the tank toppled and crashed onto the aluminium boat, partially dropping its contents into it, while saving the rest for the water where Mike was flailing his arms. The dock was on fire. I just stood there totally dumbfounded holding the net.

Martha was now heading down as she had heard the big explosion. Bill was screaming. "Where's the fucking hose?" The falling tank had thumped a crossbeam of the tool shed and it let go. The whole tool shed headed for the water. In the firelight I could see Mike with the flashlight flopping around in the water. The falling shed dragged a power cable with it tearing it out of the socket. Into the water it went with the most incredible set of coloured sparks. Just as quickly, the lights shorted out as the breakers could be heard clicking off. By now Bill had the hose and was dousing the fire. Now it was pitch dark as Mike had lost his flashlight. Fortunately, Martha had a new one with her.

"Hey Mikey," Bill yelled, "where are you? You Ok?"

It was probably all the moonshine that saved us from harm. It was certainly the moonshine that created the next scene. Martha put the light out where Mike was. He was there all right. There were dozens of trout floating around him and a lot of other smelly debris, especially toilet paper. It was me that started to laugh as Mike swam in. The rest caught the infection and we rolled on the deck. The roar must have been heard clear across the lake. "Boys," Bill said, "I think we got our limit!" That just caused another wave of laughter.

Ever since then I find it hard to get serious about fishing, could you?

SO WHO'S A WOOLY BUGGER?

It was high noon and we left the dock with an eagerness that had to get us our limits. This was our first day on the lake, and we hadn't killed ourselves to get out too early. You could see the odd boat with netting action. Mike and I decided to cruise down to the north end of the lake to try our luck. This was where the big ones were... so we were told. "Well, where to Mike?" I said, "You have had your nose buried in that fish ecology book for two days now so what are the chances of using science instead of luck for a change?" I should never have asked such a question because I should have expected the answer. The book on fish ecology seemed to spill out on the deck.

Mike looked at me with a wry squint. "I see it like this kid... the sun is high towards the south, just over that mountain. They don't like bright sun so a good area is where the shade is along that mountain. Since the air is warm, they will probably be in the lower part of the thermocline at about 40 feet down. Since rainbow trout prefer temperatures around 57 degrees, they will be at this level. There is a creek emptying into the area, over by the rock bluffs, a sure sign of a food area, particularly since there is quite a bit of vegetation there, so the oxygen will attract them. If my guess is right, I would say that the cooler thermocline intersects the underwater rock bluffs in that bay. I would say that we should troll in a deep sweep through the bay about 50 feet away from the shoreline. I'll use a willow leaf and a worm. If there is any fish in this area of the lake, then they will smell these delicious worms, because of their sense of smell. The willow leaf will also help attract them because the lateral line will pick up the vibrations and they will also be able to see the flash of the leaves, thinking they are fish. This way I am going to take advantage of four sensory organs and two instincts. I don't like using this hardware and smelly worms but Ed, I can see how this all fits together now. You can use those flies if you wish and pretend you are a cool dude but you're about to get a lesson in humility."

"That's really cool, Mike," I snorted, "but we are fishing for some little trout, and I didn't bring my downrigger with me. And neither should you expect me to scuba dive down there to measure the temperature for you. I came out here to relax with a beer and a Spratley, not get a lesson in science... anyway how the hell do you know those willow leaves will set up the right vibrations? Is that what you were doing last night... have you got some geophysical instruments in your fishing bag as well?" I was beginning to feel a laugh well-up inside as I pictured this massive downrigger on the back of this scrawny 10-foot boat. It would surely be the topic at the lodge if anyone saw it!

It was just at that moment that Lloyd's boat nudged up to ours. Lloyd stood up in the boat and lifted up this enormous 24-inch rainbow. His face beamed. He was so excited he almost tipped the boat. "My god," Mike probed, "where the hell did you catch that lunker?"

Lloyd was cool as he pointed to the sunny shoreline. "Way out there in the weeds, near the surface... right in the open. I was sitting there sipping an ale with a fly sitting on the surface enjoying the sun when this monster hit. Man, what a fight!"

"So what was the fly Lloyd?" Mike asked, "Any chance of getting some scientific reason for this?" Lloyd was pretty smug because he also got the science lesson last night. "It's got black hair and it's fuzzy, Mike... what else do you need to know? Anyway, you gave it to me... you said it was a wooly bugger or something like that and it would not work on this lake."

I could only think to myself: "*How could anyone be serious about fishing...*"

WHEN THE BEST IS THE CRAPPIEST

We were planning a trip to Whonnock Lake to get the kids to try their hand at trout fishing. Knowing that the lake was a haven for trout, this would be a great place to get the kids into a canoe and troll a line through that murky water to haul up a few of those ten inch trout. This is a round lake up on the plateau towards Stave Falls, completely surrounded in swamp except for the south end where the beach and park are found. The swamp provides an excellent place for insects and marsh life to feed the fish. And the beavers add to the scene by creating a vast marsh through the reeds and hardhack, creating neat channels to explore.

Anyway, it was a nice protected lake, and once you got your canoe out past all the beach bunnies, it was reasonably relaxing. The kids were excited at the prospect of heading out on the lake. The old man was going to show them an angling trick or two about catching trout and supper was sure to be a great meal with a mess of fresh trout.

It was about 3:00 PM when we got out on the water. The lake was placid as glass. The water was a dark murkey black from the rich algae. It was time for the lesson to start. "Now look, Shane," I said, "these trout like worms on a little spinner. What you do is hang a six inch leader behind this little spinner then put the loop through this metal thing called a swivel on the end of the line. You put a worm on the end like this, and then slip on a weight just about a few feet above the swivel. Next, throw the line over the side of the boat, pull the reel guide back so the line slips off as we move ahead. I'll tell you when you can flip the guide back. Now Sterling, it's your turn, you do the same thing on the other side of the boat." With me paddling, the two lines on either side of the boat, the kids were ready for a new adventure.

A few minutes later, the excitement exploded as Shane screamed... "Ed, I got a bite!" I tried to calm him down for fear he would flip the boat. He was like a jumping jack at the back end of the boat. "Sit down you dummy," said his brother, "don't you know anything about boats?"

"Shane, Shane, sit down and start cranking the reel handle slowly. Keep that rod pointing out and up while I get the net." A few minutes later the fish was near the boat. I didn't recognize what it was but this was hardly the time to worry about it. The kid was peeing in his pants with excitement. "Bring the end of the rod over to the back of the boat," I ordered, "I can net it here." The fish was in the net in an instant. There was no way I was going to let this fish get away. Next, a swoop of the net and a plop in the canoe and there flipped a flat thorny looking fish that looked like someone had squashed it. It was black on top and yellowish underneath. "Is that a trout?" asked Shane. "No," I replied, "I don't know what the hell it is. I'll throw it back." The next instant heard Sterling beller. "I got a bite!" Now it was his turn to bring in another one, this one a bit bigger. "Boy, that was fun Dad," he screeched, "can I do that again? Can we eat this one?" "Really, Sterl," I replied, "I don't know what these are, they must be some strange mud fish. God they look like piranaha don't they?"

It was an hour later and I had thrown away about twenty of these fish. They just would not stop biting. There was not a trout in the lake.

At 6:00 PM it was time to head in. The boys had hauled in so many fish it was old hat to them now. But still no trout. So we beached and started to pack up the canoe. Right beside us, another canoe slipped in. I could see a pail with some fish in it. Sterling asked "How many trout did you guys get, we couldn't get any?" The old guy was beaming; "Trout schmout, we got four crappies, thems better eaten fish than those crummy trout. But they's been hard to catch, we got lucky to get four. When you fillet these little guys, they's better than halibut." We all asked together... "What's a crappie?"

He reached into the bucket and hauled up a scrawny fish. It was like the smallest one we threw away. The boys looked at me and then simultaneously yelled: "We threw twenty big ones like that back in the water cause Dad said they were no good..." I walked off to the car as fast as I could. **It served me right for treating fishing as a serious matter**...

FLOATING DOWN THE RIVER WITH A FISHY ON YOUR LINE

The Chehalis River was the main target for the next salmon excursion. We knew that the salmon were making their way into the rivers as all the sports stores had posted signs telling people to head up to the Vedder and the Harrison rivers. We got together on the Friday after work. The plan was simple and clear.

Mike would stop off at the Army & Navy on his way out of Vancouver. He was itching to get a few new salmon trinkets since he had never tried salmon fishing in this river. He had always been out on the ocean dragging a fender and herring strip so this was a great opportunity for Mike to add to his inventory... after we convinced him that the fender was not a good idea on the river, that is.

It was early Saturday that the three of us met at Lloyd's place, the suggested rendezvous. As we were packing the truck with gear, Mike drove in. He was excited. "Man, have I got the stuff for salmon... come and have a look at this... there was an incredible sale at Army & Navy."

Lloyd, Les and I looked at each other and rolled eyes simultaneously, knowing full well what we were about to see. It was when he popped the trunk that we got the real picture. First, out came the waders... next came the new tackle box... then the vest... after that the new steelhead rod, reel, three books on salmon tactics, new pack, and finally the new bone dry. "Now..." Mike beamed, "look at these goodies." He then opened his new tackle box. The colours were staggering. We had never seen such an array of lures and plugs. He had everything in there. "Mike," Lloyd said, "you must have dropped a couple hundred bucks!"

"Look at it this way, fellas, you don't seem to worry about spending that much on beer and jerky do you? This stuff is all for river fishing and salmon, you jerks will be begging me for some of these beauties before the day is over."

With little else to say, we took off, finally arriving at the Chehalis Bridge 40 minutes later. You could feel the adrenalin surge as the fantastic Chehalis came into view. The fall colours, the clear emerald green waters out of the canyon... it was all too much. We were out of the truck in an instant.

"Goddamit, I got to have a beer and simmer down a bit," yelled Lloyd, "this is too much. I can feel that 10-pounder on my line already." So while he simmered down, we got the gear into the packs, ready to haul up the cliff and over the canyon to the first big pool. As steep as the first section was, it just seemed like an instant and we were on top paralleling the canyon edge, looking down into the white water below. In the distance was the first destination, an incredible deep green pool of water temporarily slowed against the sheer cliff wall. We could see the white water before and after the pool, and the gravel bar opposite the rock wall. "Jeez, that pool has to be 30 feet deep against the rocks," yelled Mike above the roar of the river, "there has to be bloody monsters in that pool just waiting for my new lure."

Ten minutes later we were scrambling down ropes on the rock wall above the gravel bar. There was no pride in who would beat who to that strategic spot at the top of that pool. Like four spiders after the same prey, we came down that cliff and ran to the river's edge. "Just suck in that clean air and give your eyeballs an orgasm," beamed Mike, "this is the life... just look at that pool!"

There was little doubt about it. This was a magic spot, and it was only one of many equally magnificent pools up river. "I think we should toss the coin for position," I said, "we can't all fish here. Let's do 20 minutes each, in rotation." I won the toss. "That's OK," said Mike, "the big ones are at the top of the pool waiting to get up the next run... that's what the guy at Army & Navy told me... so you guys can stand there and look stupid at the pool."

Just as well I thought, let the turkey test his theory. It was time to gear up and spread out. I headed for the sand opposite the deep pool while Lloyd went down and Les went up. Mike headed up to the surge of water just above the pool. His plan was to flip his plug into the white water, let it out into the head of the pool and haul it back against the current into that "school of Coho" waiting to bite at his lure. It took Mike about 10 seconds to get his rod together, pull on his new waders and snap on a red and white lure. Before we could even think about fishing, Mike had cast into the water. His problem was that the river made a circular bend at this point so even though he cast into the river, the line arched around forced by the current and pushed the lure into the shallow gravel. Mike's new strategy to avoid this was to use his new waders, go up stream a bit further and wade out into the current so he could get the lure to come back into the current, not sweep around. His engineering sense told him this was so. When we looked around, Mike had slowly manoeuvred his way 20 feet off the shore, crotch deep in the current. And this was no small feat because the current was swift as it surged over the huge boulders.

Les was the first to spot Mike and he came down to watch. I must admit I was fascinated by this quest of Mike's, so I walked over, snapped two beer and Les and I sat on a rock. Lloyd continued to be oblivious at the bottom of the big pool. Mike, positioned precariously in the current, flipped his red and white lure into the current further out and let the line go.

The line was swift to follow the current straight out to the end of the upper pool and drop into the deep green hole against the cliff. I must admit that if ever I saw a more appropriate spot for a huge fish to lurk, this was it. It all looked pretty professional to Les and I. Mike snapped the guide in place and tried to look cool because he knew we were watching. He lifted his rod to 45 degrees and started to reel in very slowly making sure the line was firm against the current.

Just as he started to reel into the lower rapids, there was this enormous jolt on the rod. The line immediately started to sing as it screamed off the reel. "I'll be a monkey's cluster," screamed Les, "he's actually got a fish." Mike could see that the tension was too light. At this rate, the bastard will be down by the bridge, he thought. From then on things happened fast for Mike. As he tried to hold the rod in one hand against the force of the fish, and reach to the front of the reel to adjust tension, he turned and lost his balance on the rocks.

In an instant, Mike was in the rapids, with his rod flailing in the air. As he surged down into the upper end of the pool and against the rock wall, Les and I just looked dumbfounded. "Shit, Ed, he's going to get sucked into the down current against the rocks, we better get down there quick." Noting Lloyd was well downstream, I screamed "Hey Lloyd, get ready to go in after Mike."

Now Mike was in the deep water. Unbelievable as it was, his rod was still in the air. Fortu-

43

nately, even though his waders were full of water, the current was so strong; it carried him along the top like a float. As we ran down to the pool's edge, we saw Mike go under, his new bone dry left on the surface. He immediately surfaced again, rod still in his hand. Now he was surging along with the current towards the end of the pool where Lloyd was.

"Bloody Hell," yelled Les, "he's headed into the next set of rapids and over the falls." Mike was just arcing into the edge of the pool and a slight back eddy. He was still holding the rod. "Mike," Lloyd screamed, "grab my line, it's right beside you... you're headed into rapids again." It was sheer luck that Mike was able to even see the line.

The fact that Lloyd had 30 pound test line on was even more of a stroke of luck. Somehow Mike grabbed the line and wrapped it around his fist. He was still bobbing in 20 feet of water, which was now starting to move a bit swifter. Lloyd, noticing Mike had grabbed the line started to reel furiously. "Drop the fucking rod, Mike and swim for Christ sake!"

This was too much to watch. We weren't sure whether to panic or enjoy the show. Les broke the tension: "Ed, there's no way he can haul him in and he's too goddam stubborn to drop his new rod. I better head out after him…" He started towards the pool, wading out into the shallows. But the line was just enough to hold Mike in place, allowing him to sweep in an arc and allowing him to reach the edge of the sand bar where he got his footing. We all just stood there dumbfounded as he stood up, Lloyd's line in one hand, the rod in the other.

Everybody had forgotten about the fish. Suddenly there he was, still in the upper pool, still hooked. The line went stiff and Mike was alive again. He started to reel, working his way towards shore. It was 10 minutes later that he was ankle deep, standing there like a pro playing that fish. It was quite a fight but Mike finally landed the monster, a 10-pound Coho.

Mike wasn't even ruffled. It all happened so fast he didn't really have time to panic. All he did was hang on to the rod. When we sat down for a beer, with that beautiful salmon laid on the rocks in front of us, Mike finally spoke smugly… as cool as Mike could say: "Guys, I knew everything was OK, I could feel that fish on the line all the way. That's why I held on. Even if I went through the next rapids, I would have held on and hauled the prick out down by the truck." We all started to

45

laugh... what could anyone say... he did catch a big fish... with his new gear... in the pool where he said they were. What we did argue about for years, however, was who actually owned the fish... Mike or Lloyd*...* **Who ever said fishing was serious...**

BIG ONES DON'T ALWAYS GET AWAY

I had been trolling a flatfish for twenty minutes. Mike was hauling in his fourth fish and it was beginning to get a bit humiliating, to say the least. The girls were beginning to roll their eyes at each other more often, trying to contain a well of giggles that were building up.

I could now only take salvation in the idea that I was out here to enjoy the fresh air and the nice company but I was beginning to think twice about the company. The peer pressure was starting to get the better of me. Leaning over to get another beer, I finally said: "What the hell is going on Mike, I am using the same plug as you are?"

Taking a side glance at the rod tip, my elder brother looked smugly at me, like the joke about the old bull and the young bull on the hill, and said: "You know, I don't recognize that vibration at your rod tip. Are you sure that you aren't dragging a beer can instead of a flatfish... Ha Ha Ha?"

Taking a look at the tip I couldn't see anything particularly strange about the wiggle on my rod tip. "So what?" I asked. "Well, kid, it's like this... pull the rod up and if you do not have a constant vibration to it then you have some problem at the other end. Maybe the wee fishy is too smart for you?" Pulling it slightly showed a smooth pull to it... but no vibration like a flatfish should have as it wiggles. After pulling it in, I could see the problem. The treble hook had caught itself on the line, completely destroying any possibility of a proper vibration. "You see, Ed, I told you to pay more attention to your rod tip and you will not waste so much time... Well girls, I've got my limit now, I guess we should go in for a while cause the kid just took the last beer. Anyway, the fish have stopped biting..."

It was at that moment that fate had its redemption. Hope had just sped the boat up a bit and Mike was reclining in his seat, smug as a bug in a rug when his rod tip showed a tug. "See that, there is a beauty sniffing around my flatfish," Mike reported, "now he is off... look at the smooth action, oops there he is again... see how you read the rod tip, Ed. He has let go again... see the vibrations."

By this time I just thought it better to humour the crowd but it really was getting to be a bit much. "Mike, you're really dreaming, that rod tip doesn't tell me squat. Where did you get this nonsense anyway, did someone sell you a book on reading rod tips?" It was at that moment that the real tug occurred on the line and the line reel screamed out of the reel. With the action of an expert, Mike lifted his rod to 45 degrees and began to reel in, cool and collected. "See, I told you guys he was toying with it didn't I. Now watch me read the line tension to keep him from spitting the hook."

We all watched in awe as Mr. Cool directed the activities. "Shit, this is a big fish... stop the motor... turn the bloody boat sideways... get the net ready." In a series of reel in and haul up on the rod to 90 degrees, Mike worked diligently at shortening the distance between his quarry and the boat. "Notice how I keep this line exactly at the same tension, yet work the bugger to exhaustion... it's all in reading the line. By now we all felt that Mr. Cool knew what he was talking about. "Man this is a whopper... this will set the record for this trip folks... we may have to make this a permanent trophy."

"Mike," I said, "why doesn't this fish break water?" "Cause I don't let him, dummy, can't you see the..." As Mike's words faded, the rest of us dummies looked at each other and began to howl instantaneously. There, a mere twenty feet out, breaking the water was this enormous black branch that Mike had expertly hauled in.

"I'll be a monkey's testicle Mike, that is going to look real good as a trophy above your fireplace. Perhaps we should inscribe a little bronze template below it saying 'how to read your rod tip'."

All I could think was: **_Serves him right for taking fishing so serious..."_**

SPARE ME THE SCIENCE... PLEASE!

Mike and I have been trolling the lake for the last hour. Every time Mike gets a strike, he jumps up like a shot and reels in. The fish surfaces and then it is suddenly gone. "Dammit, what's going on, you've landed three fish in the last hour Ed, I've lost all five!" Since Mike's line is still out, he pulls out about twenty more feet of line and sits down mumbling to himself. A few minute later, another strike! "God what a strike! This one's a whale; he almost pulled the rod out of my hand! What... he's gone!" Once more, Mike sits down in disgust and cracks an ale. He lets out 5 pulls and sits again. Five minutes later his reel starts singing. "Look at this, Ed he's huge and heading for Vancouver!" Suddenly the line went slack and Mike started to reel in frantically. His reel handle was just a blur. "Good thing you've been weight lifting those beer Mike, I've never seen such wrist action in my life!" But the fish was running towards the boat. He surfaced, took a look at Mike's ugly face, spit out the plug and was gone…

"Mike, your problem is quite simple." I laughed knowing it was my chance to tell big know-it-all brother about the technical aspects. "The problem is that you're too much for any fish to handle… its a proven genetic fact that the youngest brother in a family is always the best looking, these fish prove it. One look at you and they gag so bad they spit the hook out in terror. I would imagine that you probably look like some ancient prehistoric creature from the lost lagoon. Admittedly, their reaction is a bit severe but I certainly can't blame them for panicking…" "Oh cut the bullshit Ed," Mike interrupted, "there is definitely something wrong."

"Well if you let me finish I would tell you what's really wrong. You are loosing five fish to my one. That's a pretty poor success ratio and if you are losing them and I am not then I am obviously a much better fisherman. The best way to tackle this problem is for you to accept defeat, sit down, be humble, and let me show you how to catch fish. I'll even be happy to lie for you and tell the girls that you caught a few." I could see Mike starting to boil so I thought I better take a new attack at the old fart.

"OK OK, if you feel you're so great, then let's see you catch some fish... by the way, when did you last sharpen your hook? I heard somewhere that makes a difference." Mike looked at me with a total blank look on his face "Oh jeez, the action was so fast I didn't have time to sharpen the dammed thing." I should never have told him that because after he hauled in and sharpened it, he caught his limit and never even said thank you.

How could anybody be that serious about fishing, I thought?

BOBBING DOWN THE RIVER ON A WINTER'S DAY

It was January in the Fraser Valley and the Steelhead were reported to be running. Our phone lines buzzed as we planned the excursion. It was time to meet in Mission to plan the trip. "Why don't we go up the Chehalis River?" stated Mike with expert opinion, "I was down at the local fishing store and the owner said the lower pools just a half mile up from the canyon are filled with steelhead."

"That's a great idea," said Les, "but that's quite a climb up that canyon, particularly with a bit of snow on the ground. Why don't we take the rubber raft with us and then we can shoot down the river back to the truck... after we catch a few of those big buggers for supper." Mike's face turned blank. He just did not look as excited about that idea, but I came to the rescue. "That's a shit hot idea Les, there's hardly any snow on the ground and the water is high. We could get back down in a few minutes and avoid that climb out of the canyon. It would save us quite an effort. I'm in, let's head out in the morning."

"Just a bloody minute you guys," Mike countered, "this is winter, the Chehalis is not a nice river in winter and I've never been with you guys on a rapid run...count me out! I'll just fish in the lower pool, you guys can head up the canyon since you're such experts."

Les was first to respond. "Mike, don't be such a chicken shit, we've been down that river in this four man raft at least four times. If we put in at the fourth pool, it's an easy breeze down the rapids. Anyway, that's the hottest pool for steelhead. There's a fantastic rock ledge over this deep pool where they rest for the next rapid run. I'll carry the raft up if you're such a wimp. All you have to do is get in and Ed and I will do the rest."

The morning air was cool. Mike was excited. He had his special steelhead rod out and the new bag of fluorescent wool he got at Army and Navy. He also had a gross of spin and glo's that were on special... every size and shape imaginable. "Come on guys, let's hustle," yelled Les from the truck, "I've got the raft packed, let's boogie." So off we went.

We pulled off the road past the Chehalis River Bridge and drove into the trees along the river. The river was high. You could see the clear green water surging through the steep canyon walls, stopping briefly to form an emerald pool. A dusting of snow gave the scene an extra touch of elegance. There had to be some big steelhead in here!

Out of the truck and on with the packs, an instant later we were set to go. Mike stood there looking sheepish. "What's the problem, Mike? Still got some chicken shit stuck to your boots?" said Les. "I told you two bananas," Mike replied, "why should I believe you guys can get through there... that river looks bloody rough." The answer was inevitable. "Come on Mike, this is no different than any other time, you get a quick exciting run, then you skim through a neat pool. Three runs and you're back here. There is no problem."

Although begrudgingly, Mike followed. The prospect of those steelhead far outweighed his reservations. At the top of the bluff we stopped for a rest. The view into the canyon was spectacular. "God," Mike beamed, "am I glad I got these new steel toed boots at Army and Navy, they sure keep my knubs warm.

And these new glasses are fantastic; I can almost make out those steelhead down there in the pool below. Man is this fantastic or what?"

"Mike, just wait till we haul one out and come down the river," I beamed, "then you'll see excitement." Twenty minutes later we were scrambling down the rock ledge to the pool.

It was an hour later when we started to think about heading back. We had scoured the pools and upper edges of the runs to no avail. Those fish were not even remotely interested in us or our offerings. Perhaps they knew Mike was there. Then it was time to go. Les was inflating the raft.

"Jesus Christ, guys, that's not a very large raft. Did you look at that wave at the head of this first run... its massive. Are you sure about this?" Les was quick to respond: "No sweat, Mikey, I had a good look at it, we just have to paddle hard as we get to the end of this pool and take it on the left side. Once we get past, things simmer down through the run. By the way Mike, did you bring some sneakers or light shoes? You're not thinking of wearing those steel toed clods are you?" "Look," Mike replied tersely, "nobody is telling me to take these off, I will not get my feet wet, thank you, so these stay on."

It was senseless to argue, so we thought it best to humour him. "Hey, Ed," yelled Mike, "where are the life jackets and raft cushions?" "Shit," I replied without looking, "we've only got two cushions but there are three life jackets in my pack. Unfortunately Les and I need these at the front and back to steer the raft so unless you want to guide us through, you need to sit low in the middle." "There's no bloody way I will paddle, guys... you're the experts so I will use my life jacket as a seat."

In we got, Les in front, me in the rear, Mike sitting on his life jacket hanging on to the gear and packs. In less than a flash we were in the current. "Right side hard!" screamed Les, "That's a big mother of a wave coming up, hang on." All I recall was this huge wave in front of us, and us rising. It simply took our little raft and flipped it over.

The next thing I saw was flying gear. Les went over against the rocks while Mike disappeared. When I came up, I still had my paddle and grabbed the raft line. Funny thing was that the water wasn't cold at all. It was only an instant later that I saw old Mike bobbing like a cork to the left, new glasses gone, his steel toed boots pulling him down. He had actually flipped backwards in the current. With the raft rope hooked under my arm, somehow I managed grab him and the current shot us over against the ledge into a small back eddy. Les was standing on the other shore by now, watching the spectacle. When he saw we were all right, he started to laugh. "You guys OK," he guffawed, "man, that's what I call refreshing. That was some goddam wave wasn't it! Mike I swear that sonofabitch wasn't there last time we went down." Les looked like a drowned rat, but Mike looked a lot worse. He was dead silent. "Get on Mike, we've got to get across," I ordered. "You got to be kidding" was the subdued response, "the bloody raft is upside down." "Well I can't turn it over here so get on or swim." I yelled.

He got on, and with one paddle, we launched diagonally, turning around and around through the current, finally intersecting Les about 50 feet down stream.

"God I wish I could have filmed that, you guys would have won the white water bloopers for decades to come." Mike was hardly amused. He was white as a bed sheet. "You bastards," he squeaked, "I lost my new glasses and all my gear... and I got my feet wet... I knew you guys were amateurs, what now?" We were stuck in a canyon, sheer walls across and a nasty climb on this side. Les and I exchanged looks and said together, "There's only one way out of here buddy, and it's downstream, so let's go." By this time I noticed I was the only guy with a paddle. "Les, where's your paddle?" I asked, "Is that it way down there going over the falls?" There was dead silence. "Falls!" Mike screeched, "What the hell do you mean? You never told me about the falls."

"Mike, honest, they were not there last time, but even if we get dumped again, that's the last pool, so let's get on with it pals." I think the rest would have been imprinted in some observers mind forever, if he had watched from above. Three drowned rats, one paddle, swirling down the rapids in circles, banging against the rocks, then getting sucked back into the falls absolutely made Mike's day. They weren't big falls but to Mike they were Niagara Falls I'm sure. When we finally emerged at the last pool, Mike was sitting in six inches of water.

At the truck, it was time for beer. All we could do was look at each other and laugh. Mike was so glad to be alive he also cracked a smile. But when Les threw his beer can in the back of the truck and said: "I don't believe we got dumped by that scrawny wave... we can't go home being licked by this river, let's go back up there and try it again." Mike actually cracked up.

Who said fishing was serious, I said to myself...

EVER HEAR OF A
BOTTOMLESS BOAT?

The time was upon us when the cut-throats were running up the rivers, sloughs and creeks. We decided to head out towards the upper Nicomen Slough where we had heard the fish were as thick as thieves... looking for anything that was in the water to strike at. At least this was the story according to Lloyd, our local expert. After listening to him rant for half an hour, we gave in. After all, if this is so, we thought, then, it would be appropriate to throw a few choice plugs out into the slough to test the theory. So the usual group of fearless fishermen decided to head off with gear in hand.

"I'll tell you guys the best spot is up from the Deroche Bridge. You just cut down on the north side of the bridge then head up the bank along the slough," reported Lloyd. "Come on, man" Mike queried, "that's just a swamp..." Lloyd was quick to respond, "At this time of year the north bank is actually exposed and the channel is actually fairly clean, with prevailing moving water. I know most of the year this is normally a wide flooded area of marsh but at this time of the year a channel was actually quite discernible."

"This is a hellova great idea," said Lloyd, "we can head up to a few of the deeper channels and pools that are normally not exposed. I know a few places where the pools are actually 10 feet deep and they are close to the bank. It will be simple to huck a line out there and haul those big ones in. In fact, last year I was up there and there is actually a rapid run."

This was all a bit far fetched to me since I always remembered the slough as a wide waterway of marsh grass, not a stream, but after all, Lloyd grew up here so who was I to question his knowledge?

So we got our gear together and headed to the bridge. Off we went down into the beaten grass and along the bank. Lloyd was right. Much of the channel was actually visible and a steady flow of water was evident. After about 10 minutes we came to a wide bend where you could see a deeper hole on the other side. "Lets give it a try here," said Mike, "there's got to be bruisers in there. I'm going to try a small spinner with a worm." "Good idea Mike," said Lloyd, "I've got to have a beer anyway. We'll just watch you haul out that 2 pound trout."

"God, what a dreamer," I said to Lloyd, "I heard that some big cuts come up here but that's pretty ridiculous...." Les cut in. "No shit, Ed, there's big fish in here, you just have to use the right stuff. Let's see how the pro does."

Mike cast his spinner elegantly out into the pool, close to the overhang. He knew everybody was watching so he was trying to look really cool. It was now about 10 minutes later and no action. We had all finished the beer so it was time to move on. "Mike, you've had your chance, we're heading up stream."

After about 15 minutes of thrashing through the grass, we came to a small rise in the land. The channel was about 30 feet across and there were actually some rapids here. As we approached, you could see a deep pool below the bank as the stream made a turn against the bank in a bow. Up stream was a small run of white water. "You see," yelled Lloyd, "I told you arseholes there were rapids up here. Now isn't this a nice pool? There's gotta be some whoppers in here. I need a beer so I can contemplate which plug is going to get the biggest fish. I really don't want to waste time like Mike... got to be scientific you know..."

"Go ahead man," I yelled; "I'm heading up stream so this one is all yours." With that I forged through the weeds up past the rapids and to the next rise. At the top I noticed another fantastic pool of placid water, settled before it started its short decent down the incline to the lower pool where Lloyd was fishing away, slurping on his beer. He appeared to be more interested in his beer than fish. I also noticed this old wooden boat stuck in the mud. It was only about 8 feet long, partially submerged in the stream. The sides were all broken but there appeared to be enough wood left to it to float. Paying little attention to it, I decided to try the pool. After a few casts with a plug, it was obvious that there were no takers here so I headed further up the channel.

I could hear Mike and Lloyd thrashing through the weeds behind me, trying to catch up. "Dammit, Ed I had a bite down there. He was the most enormous fish in the place. I would have had him if Mike hadn't come through the bush like a wounded bull and scared all the fish upstream." "Piss off, Lloyd," Mike replied, "you're too pissed to know if the fish was nipping at your knackers... what a dumb story... you really expect us to believe this?"

But Lloyd was determined to give credibility to his fish story. "I'm heading up to the next pool... that's where that big one headed." Mike and I rolled our eyes at each other and followed Lloyd as he thrashed on up stream. We emerged at another wide pool. This was a nice easy flowing channel, so we dropped our gear and settled in. Lloyd was quick to get the plug out to the deeper water against the bank. Mike headed up a bit further and started selecting his flies. I just watched these two experts, sipping on my beer, chewing on a pepperoni. After about 30 minutes of flogging, I decided to rig up a float and worm so I could just sit and let chance take its turn. Lloyd was on his 10th beer by now. You could see him losing his patience.

"Hey Lloyd," I yelled, "come on and have a pepperoni before you get an ulcer. There's no bloody fish here so why don't you just admit it and cool off." As Lloyd turned around and started to say that I was right, you could see a tug on his line. He was quick to respond. "There, I knew bloody well there are big fish in here...." Then there was nothing as the line went limp. Lloyd came over and sat down.

"Well, I guess they just ain't interested. Let's eat lunch and I think I'll head back down to the lower pool."

It was about 30 minutes later when Lloyd headed down. I thought I would try the upper pool. Mike said he had nibbles back at the first pool so he was off. After I fished for a few minutes, I noticed the old boat again. I stuck the end of the rod in weeds and I went over and hauled it out. It could still float and although it looked a bit rotten, I thought it might be a great way to run the lower rapids. So I positioned the boat along the shore and went over to get my rod. "I'll just get into this boat and reel in," I thought to myself, "then I'll push off." As I got into the boat with the rod, I felt this enormous bite. The float disappeared and the line headed up stream. As I lurched to get hold and set the tension, the boat left the shore, heading straight out into the channel. "No sweat," I thought to myself - feeling adventuresome, "I'll just be cool and take this run standing up, then reel the fish in at the same time. Man will this be shit hot as I cruise by those two turkeys with a fish on the line."

In an instant I started over the run. Still standing in the boat, I started to reel in with gusto and screamed; "Hey guys, get a load of this..." Mike and Lloyd were both at the bottom pointing at me and laughing. Then I could see Lloyd disappear out of the corner of my eye. The run down was fast and to this day I don't know how I managed to maintain balance in that little boat. As I reeled in with the line straight out behind me I could still feel the fish on. First I swished by Mike who was standing on the bank laughing like he was going to split. As the little boat came in close to the bank, there was this loud crash. I looked sideways to see the front of the boat in splinters. I was now about five feet from shore but it was the longest five feet I have ever seen because when the boat started to disappear below surface, I had no choice but to try to make the jump to shore... with the rod still in my hand. These two maniacs had very swiftly decided to take a huge boulder and throw it in the front of the boat. When they saw that they had actually achieved destroying the front of it, they went insane with laughter.

Well, I did not make the shore. As I leaped out of the boat, the support was hardly enough to launch me to the bank. But Lloyd grabbed my rod as I sunk back into the channel. It was deep. It took me about twenty feet downstream before I was able to clamber out on the bank. All I could hear was the roar of these two buffoons splitting a gut as I scrambled. When I finally emerged, soaking, there was Mike rolling in the weeds still laughing. And there was Lloyd, standing there snorting like a bull in heat, reeling in my fish.

Lloyd was pretty cool about playing that fish. They were like a couple of kids encouraging each other to play the big fish. "Nice catch, Lloyd," Mike bellered, "keep him on, I'll get the net!"

When Mike netted the fish and it was on shore, they both turned around and looked at me… what a pathetic drenched sight I was. They started to laugh again. I just stood there. They laughed harder.

"Ed," Lloyd screeched, "that was quite a show… look at this big monster I just caught… that's the big bastard that got away the first time… I told you I'd get him…. How's that for skill…"

I must admit that it was funny to see these two idiots rolling in the weeds laughing. All I could think, however, was: ***"How the hell could anyone ever be serious about fishing with these two?"***

DID ANYBODY BRING THE SCUBA GEAR?

The September fall day was fantastic. It was 9:00 AM and we had rushed to get out on the lake just after the wind subsided. It had been a hot summer and the fishing hadn't been great so it was time to make up for lost time. "Well Mike, what's the prognosis today, I don't see any feeding activity... where do you suggest we start?" Mike tried desperately to appear intelligent. "Well I'd say that fall isn't here yet and it has been relatively warm so the thermocline must still be in place. It's 65 degrees and it was cooler through the night, so the surface has had a chance to cool a bit. These trout are happy at 57 degrees, that's where the oxygen is best for them."

I knew this was going to be another one of those scientific days. "Mike, why don't we just get in the boat, point it down the shore and drag some lures?" I knew the answer. He was not going to quit. He had dreamed up more ways to catch those fish. He rattled on. "So the oxygen is good at surface and there is every indication that they should be close to surface, ready to feed. Let's troll a couple of different flies just below surface. If that doesn't work then we should go a bit deeper as the sun rises and it gets brighter."

"Mike, why bother. Why not just fish? You in a rush?"

"Well, because science can help cut down on farting around the lake wasting time. This way you can get to the biting fast. There is nothing particularly revealing about this," he kept rambling, "except that the possible layer of water where the fish should be becomes a bit more predictable, simply knowing a few simple things about fish and temperature will help identify the layer where the fish are the most active."

To anybody on the lake it was obvious that the fish were around but not biting. Interestingly enough we could see a few boats at the far end of the lake where you could see the odd glitter of willow leaves. So we headed down there. "How's the fishing? " asked Mike as we cruised by one of the boats, "Pretty tough,

I've had to go to the big hardware and worms to pick up two fish in the last four hours. I hate to admit it but if I come in without any fish, my wife is going to laugh at me. I'll never hear the end of it. I've been here for two days dragging flies and plugs... I don't normally use these leaves but I'm desperate."

I could see Mike eyeballing the willow leaf, which was almost 4 feet long. He was obviously thinking about stooping to an illegal leaf. I noted two large weights. "Man you must be deep with all that lead." "Yup, but I wasted two hours dragging this bloody thing around without any weight." I finally had to kick Mike to get his attention so we could push on. "Well good luck, with your wife, we might give a few plugs a try."

"Mike," I said, "I saw you getting horney over that willow leaf. Surely you are not going to resort to that, are you?" "Not on your life, little brother, the fish were obviously not taking anything. Most of the lake is shallow, except for the far end. This was reinforced by the few fish that old fellow had caught on the willow leaves. We had been told that the lake was an average of 30 feet deep, so if the thermocline was somewhere between 20 to 50 feet deep, this would not leave too much of the lake with a desirable temperature range. In fact, the long hot summer would have forced the fish to look for deeper water. The fish would have to be down about 40 feet to get to some tolerable water temperatures, about where the willow leaf was!"

"So?"

"I definitely feel that we will be wasting our time in any area but the one deep end of the lake. The other important factor in this is that the fish will prefer to keep away from the open water so the best area would be where the thermocline is in direct contact with the steeper, protected shoreline. That area over there has a steep shoreline which looks like the water is deep, so we should troll in that area after we find the right temperature." "Sure Mike, you going to scuba down with a thermometer?" I started to laugh as I hauled in the line. Mike reached into his bag and pulled out a funny looking gismo with a reel and a funny looking probe on it. He obviously had something new that he had been hiding. "What the hell is that?" I asked. "Are you wanting an enema after those two pounds of nachos you ate?"

"Get serious kid," he snorted back, "this device allows you to drop the probe into the water, providing you with a digital read out. This is how you really want to verify this business of temperature shifts. Let me give you some simple science about water temperature." I was going to get a lecture whether I wanted it or not so I just shut up. "You see I happen to know that continued heat in summer makes the fish drop deeper as the thermocline moves lower. As the temperature cools towards fall, the water cools at surface and falls, forcing lighter water up. Then the water cools at surface, the fish come to the top to feed, also finding better oxygen levels. Because there is typically a lot of insect activity in the fall, this is the best time to try flies. As fall gets cooler, this mixing action continues, just as it did in the spring, until another state of equilibrium is reached when the water cools to 39.2. The cooling will continue until the water starts to freeze. Then the lake goes through the overturning process where the waters become reasonably mixed throughout the lake. At this time the fish will become active throughout the lake since the distinct layers of water become mixed up. The fish will tend to move to those areas which are richer in oxygen and food, rather than just those that have the ideal temperature."

"Mike, that's really helpful. How the hell are we going to find the right temperature and then get the tackle down there? Why don't you get serious?"

This was his cue to bring out his next surprise. "I know you probably are too dumb to realize what this new stuff is but its called downrigger. You use these cannon ball weights and reel to drop a vertical line down to whatever depth you want."

I had in fact seen these things as they were being used for salmon. "Now I know you're nuts. What are you going to do, club the fish with those balls? Oh, maybe you got your scuba gear in there so you can go down and club the fish." I started to laugh at my own joke.

"Ed, piss off, you can fart around at your own elevation and wait for a chance strike or you can be smart. I am going to show you how I can find those fish and where they are going to bite. I am going to head out there right where the water is deeper and the big ones are waiting to bite." What could I say? He must have spent a fortune on this stuff and he was on the motor so I cracked a Blue and sat back to watch this.

I watched him drop the thingy down to about 60 feet. He took his little engineering notebook out and started writing things down. He brought it up 5 feet at a time, scribbling stuff in his book. Of course I had to reel in while this scientific survey was being conducted. "So, Mr. Einstein, what's the verdict? Are you ready to tie a weight to your leg and go down and club one?"

"What an asshole you are, Ed. I took ten readings at 5-foot depths. The surface water temperature is 65 degrees, and then the readings were 64, 62, 60, 57, 55, 52, 49, 49, and 48. You see 57 degrees is exactly 20 feet below surface. That's where the big monsters are going to be active. That's where the oxygen is and the fish will love it there."

Well, I thought to myself, maybe he is on to something. But as I thought about this, 20 feet was about where I had been dragging stuff most of the time. Anyway, I thought, let's watch him play this out.

"OK, kid, watch the master. First you get the downrigger ready by putting it over the edge of the boat. The cannon balls go in first and you clip your line onto a release a few feet above the balls. You then drop the balls down and stop at 20 feet. As you troll, the weights keep the line at exactly 20 feet. When a fish bites, the clip releases and voila, you got a monster on the line ready to haul in. Smart isn't it?"

Well, as I thought I was fishing at that depth anyway, I put on a Spratley and let it out. Mike was now trolling with his flatfish at 20 feet. He opened a beer and sat back smugly. Five minutes into the troll, I got a strike. The silver beauty catapulted itself out of the water 100 feet back and dove. You could see the line rapidly disappear. I gripped the rod and had to tighten the tension as this monster was taking line out at record speed. It was a monster. I screamed. "Holy shit, Mike, I got a beauty! Get the net ready!" Mike bent over to grab the net and stop the motor. Just at that instant, he got a huge tug on his line. "Shit, I got one too, and I bet this sonofabitch is a lot bigger! And he's deep too so I got one of those giant ones!"

Well, we both started to crank at breakneck speed to bring the big one home. "Fuck, would you look at the rod," Mike bellered, "look at the bloody rod bend. It's going to break! Man I really have to play this whale!" I glanced sideways and I could see there was some serious stuff on his line. But like a serious fisherman, he was pretty careful to reel and pull slowly making headway. My line would slacken a bit, give me some time to haul in and then get tense as the fish ran. Both lines were now below the boat.

It was then that I noticed that as we reeled in, it was as if the lines were converging. We were both hauling and reeling vigorously and it was now a continuous pull against us. "Mike, what the hell is on this line? Where are these fish?" I screamed, "Have you still got yours on?"

"Ed, when you get a fish this big, you really have to be patient and conscious of the rod strength… as well as the capacity of the line. You go ahead and haul your minnow in first. I am still playing this trophy!"

It was about then that the lines came together. And then out of the water came some hardware. There was another line hooked around the release clip. Mike was now at surface and one 10-pound ball could be seen clearly. The fish had somehow dove and took a turn around the line by the release clip. Mike was hauling in the biggest lead fish of the day... a ten-pound cannon ball! I had nothing. While I was hauling up the ball as well, the fish threw the hook and was probably still laughing.

"Holy shit, Mike," I laughed, "you just caught yourself a 10 pound thermocline lead biter. This has to be a trophy! He's so big it took two of us to reel him in!"

I lost it. I plopped down and just let loose with yelps of laughter that you could hear right across the lake. Mike was just speechless. "I'll be a monkey's arsehole," he said finally, "can you believe it?"

After I got myself together, I could only think: ***How the hell could anyone be serious about fishing after that?***

THE ART OF SMOKING SALMON...
AND EVERYTHING ELSE

We were living on Heather Street near the Vancouver Hospital. It was an older house, built in the very early 1900's, a multiple story dwelling with not much of a yard. Mike was living on the main floor and I was going to University, occupying the basement. It was the start of a weekend and after breakfast I met Mike in the driveway. He was all excited about something.

"Ed," he said with fervour, "one of the guys at work was telling me about smoking salmon. He said the goddamdest best way to smoke is not with these little tin smokers, but with a closed insulated box, like an old fridge. Apparently the smoked salmon is absolutely unbeatable because the smoke really has a chance to permeate the meat..." I could really see the engineer coming out in Mike. Here we go again, I thought as he babbled on, what's the silly bugger going to try now? He went on "...all you do is put an electric hot plate in the bottom of the old fridge, put some alder chips in it, set the fillets on the metal racks in the fridge and 8 hours later... da...daah... gourmet smoked salmon. What do you think of that?"

"Sounds really cool, Mike, but what about the salmon... and the rest of the stuff?" I asked. "No problem little brother," he beamed, "remember the old fridge in the garage, it doesn't work anyway. The fish, well I am going to lower my pride and go buy one at the market... just promise not to tell anyone. The rest I got. Ma's old hot plate is in the garage too. I stopped off at the Army & Navy on the way home last night and got some alder and hickory chips so all I need is the fish. Plus I can use the sugar and salt recipe so I don't have to soak the thing in brine. We could have gourmet salmon and beer tonight!"

Well, I thought to myself, it all sounded pretty fine. But these schemes of Mike's seem to always turn out different than expected so I think I will stay clear of this one. All I had to do was promise not to tell anyone he bought the fish and I could get a free meal. And if I played my cards right and encouraged the old fart, I may even get the beer free. Everyone knows that a poor student can't afford these gourmet things... "Mike," I said as I patted him on the back, "let me help you get the fridge out of the garage. I've got to go out to the university but I'll be back in the afternoon."

"Shit, by that time it will almost be ready," Mike reported, "you go ahead." It was about 10:00 AM by the time we got the old fridge out of the garage. "Let's take it into the back yard and lean it against the wall of the house. That way I can reach the plug with a short extension cord." We parted about 10:30 AM.

It was about 2:30 PM when I turned north off 16th Avenue down Heather Street. I could see a ruckus in the distance. People all over and a huge fire truck parked right in the road. "How the hell was I going to get through there," I thought to myself, "what's going on?" As I drove down the street, I realized that they were parked in our driveway. Heart palpitating, I pulled in and got out. The commotion appeared to be in the back of the house. The fire hose ran from the hydrant to the back where I could see billows of smoke rising. It was only a few seconds later when the scene unfolded.

There in the back yard were three burly, enormous firemen. Two were furiously chopping this pitiful looking fridge with these huge axes. It was lying in the middle of the lawn smouldering. The third was hosing the fridge as the others slashed away, trying to extinguish any signs of fire. The door of the fridge was hanging by one hinge, all mangled. The poor fridge looked even worse. There were chunks of it everywhere as these burly fellows did their best to extinguish it from existence. I looked up to see the steaming wall. It looked like a tornado had hit it. There were chunks of stucco everywhere else but on the wall. And there on the grass was the salmon... what a beauty it must have been, now it was nothing but smouldered, charred bits all over the lawn. People were everywhere. I just stood there thunderstruck as the attack continued. Finally, one of the firemen yelled above the clamour "I thinks that's got it guys, we've got the fire out now."

It was just then that Mike broke through the crowd into the tiny back yard. "What the fucks going on?" he yelled. It should have been pretty obvious, that the fridge caught on fire, and almost ignited the house as well but I guess Mike was pretty excited. The fireman walked over to Mike and said: "Simmer down son, some silly bugger put a hot plate in this fridge and closed the door so the air couldn't circulate. God some people sure are dumb. The bloody thing got hot enough to ignite the gas and the fridge lining. Then it started on the house wall. Someone called us just in time, otherwise the whole house was about to catch on fire."

I looked at the poor gourmet fish, the poor fridge and the look on Mike's face. The panic had left the place now and the laughs were struggling to get out.

"Who are you," asked the fireman, "do you know anything about this? We need to write a report." Mike seemed very sheepish, but he was fast on the gun. "I'm the owner of the house," he said, "it must have been my brother trying out another of his experiments. Thank Christ you guys got here in time."

It was at that moment that I thought I would quietly sneak through the crowd and get him back later. *Did I want to admit that I was involved with anyone who took his fish smoking so serious?*

FISH IN YOUR SWIMMING POOL?

We had been driving for several hours now. It was time for a pit stop along the highway. As we drove through the mountains, the highway wound itself like a giant snake through the wilderness, making its way through the valley. As we came through the pass, we could see a long narrow lake in the distance. The lake glittered through the trees, sparkling its emerald blue waters like a jewel in the lush forest. As we approached the end of the lake, we could see a long shoreline of cliffs on the distant side. The highway followed the shoreline on our side, offering many park-like settings where one could reach the rocky shoreline of the lake. "What a fantastic looking lake!" Mike gasped, "I've never seen clear blue water like that before. There must be enormous trout in that lake. Let's pull off here for a pit stop and put the boat in."

As we pulled off the road towards the lake, you could see a rocky shoreline following the main road. We continued to drive a short distance to a gravel beach nestled in the trees. This offered us a nice area to launch the boat. There was not a person to be seen. "Man, I can't believe this, there is not a soul here, this is too good to be true, Ed." After getting out of the truck, we walked over to water's edge. You could see the water depth drop rapidly from the shoreline. The bottom could be seen for at least forty feet. As we slipped the boat into the water, you could see the bottom through the crystal clear water. "These fish should be able to see our plugs for miles in this water," said Mike, "this is going to be brutal!"

We fished up and down the shorelines for two hours. We tried numerous depths, and we tried everything in the fishing box, even the willow leaf. Not even a nibble. All we could get was fantastic scenery. Finally Mike could be seen losing interest. "This is ridiculous, Ed, lets go in, I've had enough scenery." As we putted in, another truck pulled up to the shoreline. This rather official looking gentleman got out of the truck. It happened to be the local game warden! Oh, Oh, I thought; now we are in shit. This lake is probably restricted. As we sheepishly got out of the boat, the warden came down to greet us. "Howdy gents, how's the fishing'?" He had a strange look on his face.

God, I thought, good thing we didn't catch anything... we will just play dumb. "I don't think there are any fish in this lake." I said, "We've been out there three bloody hours." The warden peered at us from under the brim of his hat. He had obviously noticed the Vancouver license plates on our truck. Now what, I thought. Surprisingly, the warden was very light spirited. It was obvious that this was a chance for him to have some fun and tell the two city slickers about fish ecology.

"Well, I'll tell ya fellas, this here lake is what scientists would call acidic, it ain't never had no fish in it cause there ain't nothin to eat... that's why it's so pretty and blue. There just ain't much that can grow in these rocky shores, and so nothin will allow algae to grow. If you fellers are really interested in this stuff, I got a book in the truck that explains it."

With that, he went over to the truck reached in the back and hauled out this enormous textbook. This was a strange thing for a warden to do, I thought. Flipping to the middle of the book, he handed it over to Mike. "Read that," he said with a grin. Mike started to read, not knowing what to expect.

Mike began to read: "Lakes are classified as eutrophic, oligotrophic and dystrophic. This means that the water being highly supportive, not very supportive or not supportive of providing proper fish food. It classifies a fish's relationship to food, the amount of food in the lake and how the food chain is supported. The food chain in a lake is made up of a feeding hierarchy where each larger animal depends on finding smaller edible organisms to feed on. At the bottom of this sequence is the primary food source of the smaller animals, mainly algae. Algae is the primary food of these smaller organisms, which in turn are eaten by the larger animals such as shrimp larvae and snails, and these are in turn eaten by trout. So the basic food in all waters is algae and the more algae there is in the lake the more fish you will get because the food chain is highly active and productive. Algae are visible only by the colour of the water, so the colour of the water is quite often a good indication of the classification of the lake. If we look closer at what supports algae, we find that the two most important factors are oxygen and calcium. Acidic waters have low oxygen and will provide a poor habitat because they do not promote growth of weeds and vegetation that will in turn provide an ideal environment for many forms of organic life. The green plants that require oxygen are absent so they cannot add to the supply of food, nor the supply of oxygen. Fish need to feed on the animals and insects that inhabit weeds and organic mud, where you find the larger larvae, snails, shrimp, mollusks, and so on. If these are not abundant, then the fish will resort to eating small fish including their own kind, reducing their own numbers."

Mike and I just looked at each other. Mike read on.

"The most fish-supportive lakes are the eutrophic lakes which are discoloured with algae. They are characteristically alkaline, with a pH of 7.1 and greater. They are also rather shallow. Because they usually harbour abundant insect life, there is a constant depositing of organic materials from the surface, providing plentiful bottom feed in the form of organic mud. This is also a good rooting area for plants, as well as a good place to harbour other life forms such as worms, snails, larvae, all of which will attract the fish. The water will be discoloured from the algae, being darker in appearance, making it difficult to see the bottom, even if you are close to shore."

"The oligotrophic lakes are either neutral, or slightly acidic (pH 6.9 to 7.0) They are deeper in places and are likely to have much of the shoreline dropping deeply and abruptly into deep water. Weed beds will be scattered in small areas because the acidity and the scarcity of oxygen at depth prevents their growth. Such lakes are therefore limited in food and cover. The water will be clearer indicating that there is much less algae to support the chain. The least productive dystrophic lake has a pH of less than 6.9 and will have a bare rock or sterile peat bottom, being hostile to growth of any sort. They are acidic, deep, with long lengths of sheer rock cliffs along the shore. There will be no oxygen and the water will be clear with no algae available in any forms. The least productive lake may therefore be the one that may look the best, or at least be the most picturesque. It clearly will not support the life that allows the trout food chain to exist…."

That was enough. Mike closed the book and gave it back to the officer.

"See fellers, the pretty lake is dystrophic. Guess to you fellers in the city, it would be like fishing in your swimming pools, har, har, har! You shoulda brought your pH kits from your jacuzzi, har, har, har!"

We thanked the warden for the information. Mike and I couldn't leave fast enough. *How could we ever take fishing seriously after that?*

GETTING A REAL TOEHOLD ON THE SITUATION

It was many years ago that two old Ukrainian gents used to fish the Fraser for sturgeon... back when it was still legal to do so, that is. These two old guys were so dedicated to the activity that they never had time to get married. Steve and Harry were their names. They would trundle off every Friday night after work to spend the night down on the river, waiting for that enormous fish to bite. To them it was a second source of income. Any six-foot sturgeon would bring them a few extra bucks for their enjoyment. So even though these old farts were in their late fifties, they never had time to get married. On the other hand, probably no woman would come near them for the smell of fish and their obvious lack of interest in laundry. Mike and I got to know these two gents since they played fiddle and drums in the Ukrainian band where I also played the guitar occasionally... if you could call it a band. They were known to play some good stompin music from the old country and kick up their heels at a dance once a month. Here you could down a few quarts of home brew and have a pretty good old-fashioned dance. As these old guys were also friends of the family, we got to know them quite well.

After some moonshine, they were always telling incredible fish stories about those monsters that they used to haul in late at night. The famous spot that they always headed for was the little bar opposite the tourist stand just outside of Mission heading to Hatzic. Here there was a tiny sand bar near the mouth of de Herboniez creek. You could always see Harry or Steve's truck parked on the grass. The little trail they had worn through the brush was essentially theirs. They even kept a little 8-foot wooden boat in the bush. It was so beaten up that no one but Harry or Steve would dare try to use it in that treacherous Fraser River current. I guess they figured the 100-pound test line used on their fishing gear was their ticket back to shore if it capsized. This pitiful craft was what one of them used to row out in an arc after they had rigged the hook up with eels and put a big boulder on as a weight. One of them would row out, drop the bait into the current and row back as fast as possible before the current caught them. This method allowed them to get the line out quite far, much further than if they tried to cast it. One would then row back while the other held the rods and they would religiously set up the tent. They then hauled out the garlic sausage, home brew and proceeded to play cribbage until the fish would strike.

One evening when the two of them were over at our parent's house in Mission, the fish stories flowed in profusion. These were such incredible experiences that Mike and I were glued to these two, goading them on. They gave vivid descriptions of how they took hours hauling line on their shoulders pulling these enormous alligator like fish out of the water. Sometimes they had to both work at these fish pulling back and forth up the bank to eventually tire the monsters. They told stories about tying the line to the flexible small cottonwoods to play the fish back and forth. It was pretty incredible to listen to this.

It was inevitable that we would ask them if we could come with them on a Friday and stay with them overnight... hopeful that we would see one of their experiences first hand. I remember the look on the two playful old fart's faces when they agreed.

The condition they told us, was that we could not bitch about the mosquitoes and that we would have to get our own eels... dug out of the marsh ditches along the Silverdale Flats. Third, we needed a sturgeon bell, 100 pound test line and a rod and reel as big as we could find. We would bring our own tents and we could all play cribbage. Fortunately we knew how to play it. They said they would bring the food, booze and hooks, and show us the ropes. This time they were heading out on Saturday and staying overnight so we would have a chance to come out from Vancouver and get our stuff on the Saturday.

Needless to say, this was pretty exciting a prospect for us to learn from these two old hermits. They were always catching fish because they used to bring our mom the occasional chunk. So we knew that these two were no pikers at fishing... after all, they had been doing it for at least 10 years.

The adventure began in the morning on Saturday. We knew by this time that the eels were in the mud in about 1-2 feet of swamp water beside the Lougheed Highway on the way to Ruskin. You had to get down the bank into the ditch in the bull rushes with hip waders and dig out a chunk of hard mud. The little critters would wiggle and squirm as you pulled them out of the mud and into the container. I was surprised to see these things up to 10 inches long and they made one a bit queasy. Mike was especially chicken shit about it and refused to get into the swamp. I persevered until I encountered a huge black bull snake staring at me through the weeds. I didn't know these ominous creatures were harmless at the time so we both froze. When he slithered back I got the hell out of there as fast as I could. All Mike could say was he was sure glad he wasn't there or he would have shit in his waders and never lived it down. I knew that was true and the prospect of him telling Harry and Steve about why he had turds in his new waders was even funnier.

So we headed for the little parking area. We had our bucket of eels and our steelhead rods. Mike had gone to the Army & Navy and picked up a complete outfit for the occasion... rod, reel, line, huge hooks and other stuff the guy told him were essential. He must have dropped a hundred bucks but Mike said it was worth it. My gear was not quite as sophisticated but I thought it would be better for me to watch and learn for the next time.

As we pulled in, there was Harry's truck in the usual spot. It was about 4:00 PM when we got out onto the little sand bar. There they were playing cards sitting on a couple of old rickety aluminium chairs. Now their English was not the best. "Alloh boys," motioned Harry in his broken English, "how, you guys are today? Ve already gots two bitings from beeg buggers out in river but still no catch it one." When I saw their fishing gear, I thought wow, that's pretty shabby but I guess it's well used. Man, were they ever impressed with Mike's new gear.

After they simmered down and poured a shot of moonshine, it was time for the lesson. It took about 20 minutes for them to show us how to hang on a big rock, put a huge hook on the leader and poke those poor eels several times to create a squirming ball at the end. Then Steve took his hatchet and cut a few crutched branches, sticking them in the mud about 30 feet back from the river. "I show it for you guys... you watch it close. Da rod it be resting on da branch like dis. Now Harry, you take boat and get out in river wit hooks." Harry got in and pushed off up stream in this thing that I would be afraid to put in a frog pond and oared his way out into the river in an arc. Once out about 150 feet, he threw the first line in. The 5-pound rock sank quickly. Next out went Mike's and in came the craft. Steve put the rod up against the crotched stick and hung a bell to the rod end. "You see guys," he said, "ven feesh bite, bell ring and you grab rod. If fish too beeg for rod, ve all grab rod and line and haul the bugger in. Now ve can take easy make nice card game... have some kolbasa and nice whiskey ve make it this year."

Well, the time went fairly fast after a few snorts of that white lightning. I could see how they could tolerate those millions of mosquitoes. Only a few hearty mosquitoes would dare bite for fear of an overdose of garlic and alcohol. The card game added to the speed of the night. No one paid much attention to the rods. At 9:00 PM it was time for a fire... to warm up the sausage. Time to set up the tent. They had a ragged piece of canvas strung over a branch while we set up Mike's new tent. Still no action on the lines.

It was about 9:30 when Mike asked, "What happens when you get a bite at night and you can't hear the bell ring?" Harry looked sideways at Steve. It was time to have some fun. "Vell, ve sometime tie a string to beeg toe so if fish biting, we can feel 'em and run out to get rod." Somehow it was hard to visualize this in the pitch dark but I wasn't the expert, and Mike was taking it all in. "Steve like to tie string to finger but not me. If fish bite ve grab it pole before lose it in river. Today I tink I listen for bell and have whisky for nightcaps. For you Mike, we tink you need to tie line to beeg toe." You could see the two old farts giggling but it made sense. After watching Mike tie the thing to his toe, I thought I would just rely on hearing the bell. It seemed pretty odd but I suppose it would certainly work.

It was about 11:00 PM, pitch dark except for some dim moonlight, when I was rudely awakened. I remember a bell, then a yell, and another. Next there was a flurry of action and the tent tore off as if some fierce animal had run through it. I could see the mass of the tent thrashing about five feet away. Then the screaming started. Dazed, I just stared at the furor wondering what the hell was going on. Then Mike started to really yell. "Fuck" he screamed, "I can't get out of this goddam tent… I can't see… fuck, there's a fish on this goddam line. My toe… my toe... help you dumb bastards… where the fuck are you guys?"

By this time Harry and Steve were out of their

tent. They were trying to unravel the ball of the tent. Now Mike started to scream in pain. "Jesus Christ, my fucking toe is caught and the fish is hauling the rod out." True enough, I could hear the bell ringing and the rod silhouette was definitely not there. Steve was tugging at one end of the tarp while Harry was yanking the other end. Mike was still screaming. "Holy smokes" yelled Harry, "der is beeg fish on line... grab line fast... ver da hell is bloody rod?" The next scene was a beauty. Steve had pulled the tent off Mike who was still bellering like a bull. As the light moved from Mike, I could see Mike's rod stretched out, the line on his big toe. The line was as tight as barbed wire straight out to the river. The other end was still on the reel. The picture became instantly clear. Mike had carefully taken slack line between the reel and the first rod guide, pulled out about 30 feet of line and looped it several times around his big toe.

This was obviously Mike's grand plan. Having his toe between the fish and the reel, Mike figured that the tug would wake him up, slip off the toe and give him a chance to run to the rod. If he were really fast, he would be able to get to the rod before the 30-foot loop became tight. Unfortunately, the loop on his toe got snarled at night while Mike was snoring and the tug tightened itself firmly. Now the fish was firmly and directly hooked to Mike's toe. It was no wonder he was yelling. Well Harry grabbed the rod but Mike's toe was holding the fish so both Mike and the rod were pretty useless accessories.

"Shit, Harry, vot ve do?" yelled Steve. "Grab da bloody line" yelled Harry. It was obvious that the 100 pound test line and that fish had every intention of hauling Mike into the water. Harry managed to grab the line but this fish was off like a rocket. "You grab line too," bleated Harry, "dis sonofbitch is beeg one, I can't hold dis goddam line!" By now some of the tension was off Mike's toe as we grabbed the line. Mike was trying frantically to get the knot off the toe but it was cinched nicely. "Fuckin' hell, Steve, dis be very beeg fish, ve don't vant to lose da basturd." Now it was quite a scene as the silhouettes moved up and down the shore. First you could hear instructions to haul up, then forward, all the time yelling to get the line off Mike's poor toe.

I am not sure how Harry and Steve actually played that fish to exhaustion but they did. It took Mike about ten minutes to get the line loose. By this time Harry and Steve had a routine, automatically walking back and forth in the moonlight as the fish tried to run. Finally the line was free and Harry grabbed the rod. They had obviously figured out the whole thing. It was fate that that fish was well hooked. An hour later, they literally hauled together up the bank and beached the monster. When we went over with the flashlights, there was this six-foot sturgeon, looking like a pre-historic crocodile. The real frenzy started when Mike hobbled over and yelled "Holly shit, I caught a big one."

I don't know how long we laughed, but my abdominals ached for a week after. To this day, when I think about that night, I always remind myself that there is **no way that anyone could really take fishing serious**...

BIG ONES ALWAYS COME OUT AT NIGHT

We had been fishing most of the evening with little success. It was a pleasant enough evening, with a slight breeze skimming the water, creating patches of ripples here and there. But the coolness of the evening was beginning to chill the bones. The sun was now down and the dusk was slowly consuming the light of the day. The girls were getting restless. They had tucked their books away.

"Well folks," Mike yawned, "it's time to head in for the day, let's reel in and head for the cabin. A nice glass of port by the fire would be my choice right now." It was getting dark now, but the sky was light enough to see silhouettes of the landscape above the dark waters. You could hear the loons shrill across the lake. Three boats were sitting still in the lagoon just over to our left side. You could just barely make out the image of fishermen standing up

103

in their boats, and you could hear the familiar sound of fly reels breaking the evening silence. "Ed these guys are fly fishing! I've read about these fish and their seeing ability that changes at night. It's pretty dark, how the hell do they expect a fish to see a fly being trolled?" Just then a faint plop was heard behind us. The ripples in the water could be seen as the lighter sky reflected off the wave pattern. "Man, they've started to surface, Ed, we can't go in now... they are coming up for the flies. How the hell can they see them? They must recognize silhouettes against the sky, lets just troll a Tom Thumb on the water, really slow."

"Guys," Mike said seriously, "I never really thought about this but now I remember a section in my fishology bible on this topic."

Now I knew we were in for some serious information again. He started his spiel; "Apparently fish have a highly developed ability to see in such a way that they can switch from day to night vision because the fish eye contains rods for night vision like a cat and cones for day vision. The cones are the colour receptors for day vision, sensitive to bright light. The rods are sensitive to dim light, able to allow seeing in the dark. Humans also have rods and cones except that fish have many more rods for super light sensitive sight at night. The rods, which are about 30 times more sensitive than cones, are only capable of black and white vision, but they are very capable of seeing in dimly lit waters that exist at night or at depths in the water. But that's not all. The fish has another most unusual vision ability. It can switch from day vision to night vision automatically. This process, which is initially triggered by a setting sun, may take a few hours before the rods are operating at full capacity. As they slowly shift into position, close to the retina surface, they begin to provide enhanced ability to see in the dark for several hours. After that, the rods start to slowly retract back to their recessive positions away from the retina.

During the evening, just before total dark, when the rods give fish excellent vision, they are likely to change their feeding habits. Because the rods do not distinguish colour, fish will go after hatches of insects on the surface, or after other bait just below surface with an acute accuracy. They will typically not go after anything unless it appears as a recognizable silhouette against the darkening sky, so colour is of no significance. If the moon rises, then the acute vision will continue. They can stalk their food very efficiently in marginal light. At night you may even get some continued feeding activities, particularly if the sky has any light in contrast with the dark water, but typically, the feeding will slow down during heavy darkness, to be reactivated again in the morning light. So there guys, this is a hot moment that we need to take advantage of."

I had to admit these fish were active. You could hear the girls sigh in discontent. "Just how do you expect to tie a fly on in the dark Mike?" Hope asked, "You can't even see your beer can." But Mike was not one to be thwarted easily. Out came his special little flashlight. "Hold this while I find the right fly." he giggled.

The moon was now above the mountain behind us. It really was a remarkable evening. All around us you could hear the fish rising. You could see the ripples as they rolled into the surface water. Mike had the fly on in a flash, and out the line went. "OK let's cruise along this shoreline." he said. We sat quietly as the boat skimmed across the dark still water. Just as I was about to side with the girls and tell Mike to stop fooling around, Mike let out a squeal of significant volume. It was quickly followed by the scream of the reel.

Now the pace quickened and the fish apparently came closer to the boat. I got the task of netting. It was really dark now and I couldn't even see the edge of the boat. "Holy shit, there is a bloody whale on the end of this line guys, are you going to just sit there or net this goddam thing?"

The events that followed are embedded in my memory forever. All I remember was taking a swat at the water where I thought the fish was. The clatter of gear and beer cans was heard as the swing missed the water and I lost balance, twisting sideways into the bow. The high-pitched screams must have been heard all the way down the lake, fortunately covering up the big splash as I hit the water.

"Where is that silly bugger?" screamed Mike, "How the hell am I supposed to keep this thing on the line and concentrate with you making such a fuss?" If I could have grabbed him and pulled him, I would have, but the girls screeches were now even louder... "Where's Ed. Christ, he's in the water, I can't see anything..."

Well I could at least feel the boat after I surfaced, so I just held on to the rail and sheepishly whimpered, "I'm here guys." I must admit getting into the boat was probably the most hilarious thing anybody could have seen… if they could see it. It certainly wasn't very funny to me. Even when we started the motor and headed home, Mike was still holding onto that fish. At the dock, believe it or not, the fish was still on. We all headed for the cabin while Mike tried to haul it in. It was half an hour later when Mike finally came into the cabin, with this scrawny eight-inch fish. We just looked at each other and started to laugh…it was something we remembered for *some time after. That's when I knew for sure that* **there was no way fishing could ever be serious**.

GRANNY GIVES A FISHING LESSON

We had decided to take our mother out with us for a troll across the lake. Sometimes you just feel those pains of responsibility and you do these silly things. Even though she was in her 70's, she was quite a spry old bird and she was really quite keen about the idea of coming up to do some fishing with us. In fact she was so keen that she had gone to the local sports shop to buy some lures. How the hell could anyone turn that down? Us experts would just have to live with this and give her a nice moment. Fortunately she couldn't get to the Army & Navy like my brother could and buy everything in sight so I thought she would get some conservative lures and flies. She thought that it would be a surprise for us and also thought that it would be a nice gesture on her part. So she tucked her little bag of what she thought the fish would like in her suitcase.

We packed up the group and headed north from Vancouver. We decided to head for Pillar Lake for the weekend because of the unique rafts. These were flat rafts with 4 or 6 lawn chairs on the deck and a 9-horse kicker on the back that really allowed you to recline with beer and rod to put-put around the lake in supreme comfort. With a guardrail around the perimeter, this was the perfect vessel to keep old ladies out of harm's way.

The excitement mounted as we headed for the rafts after we got unpacked at the cabin. The big issue was who was going out with granny for the first day. Eldest brother Mike won the toss but he said I had to come so he could manage the motor. It wasn't worth making a fuss so off we went. I could see her clutching this huge brown bag as she got on the raft. Mike started the motor and off we went to the hot end of the lake. We picked a time that we knew was going to be good, to thrill the old lady for sure. Mike picked up the rod and said: "Well Mom, what do you think you should use to catch these trout?" Wrong question.

That was the perfect cue for the old girl. "Mike, I bought some stuff back in White Rock, this really nice fellow told me what I should buy for trout. Here they are in this bag." Mike glanced at me with a peculiar grin, rolling his eyes as he took the bag and proceeded to dump the contents on the floor. "Wow," Mike snorted, "I've not seen stuff like this for years!"

The colours were actually bizarre. There were colour mixtures that would give Van Gogh a headache! Mike started to laugh. I couldn't contain myself either. "Mom, that was really nice of you but I don't think these fish have ever seen stuff like this, are you sure you want to try these?" It was really difficult to keep from rolling off the raft. I would never have believed this kind of stuff could be found in a sports store. How could anyone sell this stuff to an innocent old lady? Mike was actually inspecting the trinkets with interest.

What was making it even harder for me to contain myself was that now I knew where my brother had picked up these genetic traits and I was wondering why he laughed. God, like mother, like son... both of them were like the packrat after colourful trinkets. They both had little respect for what the fish really wanted... it was what they liked. Mike picked up a long thin thing that looked like Christmas tinsel. It had twists in it like a candy cane and some florescent fuzz sticking out in three rings. The line of three hooks was hanging below it. That broke us up. Mike and I lost it.

Fortunately, the old girl was well endowed with a sense of humour so she started to laugh at us laughing. "You guys are so funny," she said, "what's wrong with you anyway?"

"By the way, Mom, what's in that other bag?" I gasped, after my rib cage started to hurt. I had noticed this other brown bag. Very carefully she picked up the bag and opened it. Reaching in she hauled out a few chunks of garlic sausage and a small knife. It was obvious that the Ukrainian blood was now really coming through. Dead silence. Mike and I just looked at each other.

"Well you see, it's like this boys, it's for me and the fish. I have some cheese too. You didn't expect me to bring worms did you? I think those fishes will like this food too…" I didn't have any more laughs left in me. It would hurt too much. "Mike, for Christ sake, stop it already. My sides are killing me, we'll scare every fish in the lake." "Shit, it won't matter," he guffawed, "those fish won't be able to resist these beauties!" Well, once more we just heaved with giggles.

Totally ignoring us, she picked up a gnarled lure that looked like a Christmas candy cane. "The nice man said this one would catch big ones... it cost me 8 dollars!" Mike and I could only stare as she hacked off a chunk of garlic sausage and stuck it on the three-barbed hook. "Mike, you put this in the water for me," she ordered. "Ma, that's such a big lure we are going to give you the big rod so when you catch that monster down there this steelhead reel and 20 pound test line will make sure you get him." Mike did a rolling eye glance at me and hid a giggle welling up again. This was too much. "How deep are you going Mike?" I goaded, "You surely won't need any extra weights, will you?"

I just had to settle down. It was time for me to have a beer and let my own line out. I just quietly put on my blue flatfish and three weights, letting my line out as silently as possible. "Ed," she said, "do you want to try one of mine, I have lots of sausage?" I was quick to respond, "No thanks Mom, I already have my line out."

Well you probably know the rest of the story. It was less than 5 minutes gone by when that 20# line straightened out like a line on a harpoon. "Mike, I got a fish!" she yelled, "What do I do now?" At first I thought she snagged a stump but when this silver monster propelled itself about three feet out of the water a hundred feet out, the whole picture changed instantly. "Holy shit, there's a fish on there." Mike and I said simultaneously.

"Ma, just reel it in... turn the handle... no, no, the other way... wait, let me set the tension... no, hold your rod up..." It was pretty futile telling her what to do because she was so excited. It was fortunate that she had this steelhead rod and the heavy line because it really didn't matter what she did wrong. The fish was really hooked well, and with this crank handle about eight inches long, Granny made short work of that six-pound monster's energy level. She just hauled him in like he was on a winch line.

I am sure everyone on the lake heard the excitement. There was so much squealing and yelling, other boats came around us to watch. Mike netted the fish. The boats applauded and cheered. I must admit I was just dumbfounded. This was a big fish. It raised so much attention, one of the boats came over and the guy asked: "Lady, that's really something, what were you using to catch that beauty?" I am sure when he saw the steelhead rod, he was a bit bewildered.

"Well," she replied, "my son helped me with the hook and bait. He can tell you." It was indeed a funny thing to see my brother explain this one to the guy. I have to admire him for that because he did it with a straight face. But it was even funnier when Mike very sheepishly looked at his Mom and said: "Ma, what else have you got in that bag?" How, I thought to myself, *could anyone ever be serious about fishing?*

WHO SAID FISH DON'T PREFER COLOUR?

We were all sitting around the crackling fire sipping a cool ale, reminiscing about the day's events. The day's fishing had been quite an adventure, with our mother catching what had to be the most massive fish we had ever seen on this lake. "I still can't believe what I saw," I said, "there is absolutely no logical reason why Granny's bizarre lure with its combination of colours and the chunk of garlic sausage drew in that enormous fish."

"You know I've been disturbed by that as well," Mike reported. "so I actually found my fishology bible that I picked up at the Army and Navy and was reading about fish and colour while I was in the can." "Mike," I said, "give me a break." Mike was quick to respond. "Look, you caught bugger all today so shut up and listen. If you can keep quiet for a few minutes, I will do the honour of giving you some real inside stuff on fish." What could I say? The beer and the fire were nice so what the hell? Let us hear the entertainment.

Mike went over to the bedroom and came back with a completely dog-eared book that looked like it had been used in the can, never mind read. "Where have you been hiding that beauty, Mike?" I snorted, "It certainly looks like it's been used... the number of fish you've caught sure isn't a reflection of the number of times you've opened that book!" Mike just leered at me and told me to shut up and listen. He started to read:

"In the previous section we mentioned that trout have the ability to distinguish colour - probably as good as our own ability. This means that a fish will identify potential food on the basis of colour in addition to identifying food shape and size. Although the trout has good colour vision, he must deal with a problem that is not one of his own doing, but due to science. This relates to how colour is absorbed by water. Fish begin to lose the capability to distinguish certain colours not because of their seeing ability, but because of what water does to light. At night, colour simply disappears and the fish sees in black and white. During the day, what the fish sees will depend upon the clarity of water and the depth of the water from where the fish is viewing the object.

In clear water for example, almost all light, or about 99% of it, is gone at about 30 feet below surface. By 40 feet, all light is gone. Water clarity, or turbidity, has even a more dramatic filtering effect on light. If the water is murky, all the light can disappear within 10 feet of surface. Needless to say, if there is very little light then not only will it be difficult to see colour, it will be difficult to see at all. Nevertheless, because of their superior rod seeing ability, fish require very little light to see well and can see well enough to feed at depths where the light is supposedly gone.

If you can once again remember your high school science, you will recall that the normal white light we see contains all the different colours. The colour you see on an object is the one that is reflected to your eye, the others are absorbed by the object. Similarly, colour is actually absorbed by the water, some colours faster than others, leaving the rest for you to see. If you look at a rainbow (the colours in normal white light) you will see how colour changes by shades starting with violets, blues, then greens, yellows, orange and red in a predictable fashion. Each colour has a specific wavelength and the reds are the longer, then get shorter as the colours change towards the blues. Water has a tendency to absorb the longest wavelength colours the fastest as normal light, which contains all colours, tries to penetrate deeper, the reds become diffused quickly - within 30 feet. The next ones to disappear are orange, then yellow and so on. The shorter the wavelength, the deeper the colour remains a colour, simply because less is absorbed by the water.

The blues can therefore be seen clearly at greater depths while the reds will just appear as a dark shade of grey. This absorbing process will have a tendency to alter the colour characteristics of light below surface. It has a rather dramatic effect on what colours are actually seen by the fish at the various depths. Water absorbs reds the fastest so that by 30 feet red cannot be seen. Blues and greens are the slowest to be absorbed. A bright red lure would be bright red at surface but at 20 feet a pure red lure would not reflect reds and appear as colourless black. If the lure were blue, then it would appear blue to the fish even at 30 feet. But if you had a lure that was a mixed blue and red at surface, the red would begin to change into a grey tone as it went deeper, finally appearing black. The resulting mix would be as a blue-grey, moving to a blue-black, creating a much different colour than you would expect. You may have expected the blue and red to make purple but that is incorrect. If you are a diver, you will already know this. Although blues and greens last the longest, being visible beyond a hundred feet or even more in clear water, there is a depth at which everything appears blue. This is because the light isn't there at all. In this situation a blue plug will not show up, as it will blend in with the blue surroundings. So there is not much sense in thinking that a nice red plug will be seen as red 20 feet below surface. On the contrary, it will only be seen as a dark shade of grey."

"Now let us add another complication. If there is a high concentration of suspended matter in the water, the whole process is reversed. The blues go first and the reds last! This process is most evident in waters that are discoloured from pollution. When this is the case, you would need to use reds and yellows to show off your lure…"

I couldn't listen to this any longer. "For God's sake, Mike, how in the hell could any normal person make any sense out of that? That could confuse Einstein..."

This was Mike's cue. "Well, for dummies like you, I can simplify it for you. Here's the dummy version."

"Think about three simple things, depth, darkness, and water cloudiness increase... as they increase so will the tendency to lose the red end of the colour spectrum. For example, consider the increasing darkness (at dusk) and increasing light (at dawn). At dusk the reds disappear the fastest and at dawn the blue-greens are the first to be seen. As you go deeper, you also see the reds disappear the fastest, leaving the blue-greens to be visible. As water clarity increases, this process simply accelerates. So if you want to show colour, and the colour that you are displaying is supposed to be recognized by the fish, then be aware of the depth, water clarity and the colour before wasting too much time. Those dazzling lures lose their dazzle very quickly in water."

The fact was that Mom's lure was about 20 feet below surface, where the reds, oranges and yellows had almost disappeared. At that depth, the greens and blues would show up the best, and anything else would just show as grey tones so the lure's colours didn't show to the fish even if he could see colour. In fact the water was fairly turbid with algae so my guess was that the red to yellow colours were gone within 5 to 10 feet. To me the key was more in the clear shape of that lure that simulated a recognizable prey.

I just couldn't resist this. "Mike. What horse-shit! That's your scientific synopsis? I personally think that fish was so big she just dragged it over him and pissed him off so he bit. On top of that, he must have been a Ukrainian fish who finds it impossible to reject that garlic sausage." I had to laugh at my own joke. As I was guffawing, it got the girls roll-ing. Mike just stared at me. Mom broke the scene.

"Boys, boys," she said sternly, "that nice man in the sport's store said he was an expert. He said that one would work the best. I think you boys need to go and talk to him instead of reading all that funny stuff."

Mike and I looked at each other with a blank look as everyone waited for the big response. He put his book down, picked up his beer and turned on the radio. It was a good thing because it drowned out all the giggling. ***There sure wasn't anyone else around here that thought fishing was serious.***

VAPOUR TRAILS MAY NOT BE SUCH A SILLY IDEA

I was having a great time hauling in fish. Now I was letting the small ones less than 2 pounds go. Mike was using the identical lure, the same weight and he was trolling at the same depth. Yet after an hour he was not even getting a nibble. "I've seen this before," Mike said, "I must be sending these fish some bad vibes, what the hell is wrong? It is really difficult to understand why these dumb fish would discriminate between the two identical situations. I could believe this if you had caught just one fish, but this defies the laws of probability."

Poor Mike, he was really befuddled. I couldn't resist the opportunity. "Mike, the only thing I can say is that these fish are a lot more discriminating than you think. It must be all the beer, pepperoni and garlic you ate last night... I'll just bet they are sensitive to the vapour trail you are leaving behind you on your side of the boat! I don't mind telling you that if I were behind you I would certainly avoid you... Wow! Feel this baby go! Look at him take line!"

After I hauled the beauty in, I snapped an ale open and laid back. It was my chance to give my older brother some information. "I was reading once that smell is a long distance sensing device to a fish. This is a highly developed ability which they can use to smell food or danger. Their nostrils contain highly sensitive apparatus that can detect incredibly minute particles in the water as it passes over the sensing organs. It is reported that this is how migrating fish are able to 'smell' out their place of birth. Apparently these fish noses are quite capable of smelling minute traces that even many scientific instruments are incapable of detecting, so they are able to smell their way back home..."

Mike rudely interrupted my spiel. "Ed, do you expect me to believe that crap? Where did you read this anyway?" I could not resist this one. "Well, my dear brother, it happens to be a chapter in that book you have been reading that you call your scientific fishing bible..."

There was dead silence. It was hard to contain myself but I took the opportunity to keep talking. "It says that the interesting part of many studies done on this topic is that the fish also has this ability to memorize minute combinations of odours, as they appear to do in the case of migration. The ramification is that this capability gives a fish the ability to discriminate between odours, and what they belong to. In fact several hundreds of odours can be discriminated on. This makes it possible for the fish to discriminate between predators, types of food, other fish, soil or mud types, types of vegetation, males or females, and probably a wide variety of things that we are not even aware of, let alone believe. In many tests conducted, it has been concluded that fish are even able to smell distress or danger."

"What this all means is that the ability of the fish to smell and discriminate so many different situations makes it difficult to fool them. In addition, since this a long range sensing device, they are able to detect and avoid hostile situations well in advance. The fish may reject a plug that has no familiar odour, or it will shy away from the odour of dead fish, or even man's touch. Something as harmless as handling the lure may be picked up by the fish and immediately recognized as a foreign smell. And when you are trolling, you will be leaving a 'trail of odour' behind you for the fish to pick up. On the other hand, a recognizable smell can be detected at long distances away, so this can work to your favour. Since the fish relies heavily on smell to seek out familiar food, offering live bait of a familiar variety, or artificial bait with a familiar odour, may be the most effective fishing tactic." I could not resist the next statement. "Mike, I really think that you've had the gear too close to your butt and all those pepperoni farts have contaminated the tackle. With all the sensory sensitivity, what fish would ever choose to bite such a terrible odour?"

Mike just sat there puzzled. "That is really cute, Ed, I still think it's horseshit. Do you really expect someone of my intelligence to believe all that? I refuse to try another plug. Maybe I'll just reel in and sharpen that hook again." As Mike began to reel in, I had to ask; "By the way Mike," I said, "how many times have you sharpened the hooks on that plug today? What's the point of sharpening the hooks if they aren't biting at them? I remember reading something in one of the Angler's Almanacs that said that fish can pick up the smell of humans from hooks if they are handled too much." Mike looked up with a perplexed look. "You're right, I've sharpened the hooks 3 times in frustration, but that's still hogwash Ed."

"By the way, Mike, the solution is even better," I countered, "the book said that if you spit on the plug, the saliva will not only get rid of your smell, it will attract the fish..." Mike was quick to respond; "You know, I've never heard anything so dumb before. I think I will do it just to prove you wrong!"

So Mike spit on his hook and let out the line. Well, guess what? Mike was still in the process of letting line out when the big five-pound trout hit! ***I can't believe that anyone would ever say that fishing was a serious matter.***

WHOSE GOT THE RIGHT VIBRATIONS?

This lake was a new adventure for us. We did not know the lake well and it was really hard to read. Perhaps the combination of weather and lack of relevant tactics were the reasons for poor productivity. The lake was a dark blue-green colour, obviously full of algae. It had to be a good lake with ample food in it - perhaps too much food. We had tried just about everything that a sports fisherman could try, with little success. Where were they? How many days did we need to end the drought? "I really don't understand this Mike," I said, "are we being punished for something we did? The only thing left to try is dynamite. There has to be fish in this lake, maybe we should forget this place."

Mike started to rummage through his box. He was obviously looking for something. "I think that we aren't being smart enough. We have been dragging different flies at different depths, but we need to take better advantage of the fish's abilities. The other factor is that this lake is so dark that these fish must not be able to see more that 2 or 3 feet. We need something that will bring these fish to us. Obviously trying to find them isn't working, let's get them to find us." I was mystified, had my brother gone bananas? What did he think we had been doing for two days? Since when did fish come to us? "What do you propose Mike, dragging a mermaid behind the boat? You got one that looks like a trout hidden in there?" Mike kept digging in his box, finally emerging with two packages. I was obviously going to get some new secrets out of my older brother.

"Little brother, I have two things here that we need to use. The first one is for you, it's called a buzzer, and the second is a three-foot willow leaf. This buzzer I found in this funny little shop in Washington. It is supposed to set up a vibration as you troll it. I have no idea what this vibration is supposed to simulate but it is supposed to set up a rhythm that induces a curiosity in fish, probably like the buzz bomb. These fish use the lateral line like a sonar device so if this sound is even the slightest bit interesting they will come in to see it. Now I have no idea what kind of bug thing this is supposed to be so that's where you enter with your willow leaf. The gold colour should show through this water, and the spoons should also set up a vibration and look like a school of fish. You should drag a yellow plug since that will show best in these blue-green waters. And we should not go too deep, say 10 feet?"

"Mike," I said, "you just never quit do you? Where did you hear about this crazy theory?"

"Ed, crack me a Blue and I am going to read you some really shit hot stuff I read a few weeks ago. I've got the book here. Sit down and listen. Well, I had heard this before many times. This guy always had his brain cranking when it came to trying to outwit those dumb fish. Anyway, I thought I might as well humour the guy. He started to read.

"The next highly developed long range sensory mechanism in the fish is its sound system. The fish hears sound underwater exactly as we hear sounds above water. The big difference is that the fish's hearing ability is amplified by the fact that sound travels about five times faster in water than it does in air. The fish will hear a splash on the water five times faster than us if we are the same distance away from the source. Fish are also capable of hearing a wide range of sound frequencies almost in the same range as humans. Fish do not have an ear drum so the sounds are received directly, making reception quite effective for long distances. In addition, the fish can distinguish different sounds just as we can, acting appropriately depending on whether the sound is familiar or foreign. A foreign sound will make the fish head for cover, as will a sound, which is recognized as being associated with an enemy. A familiar sound however will attract the fish. Very much like the other sensory devices, the sound is used to seek out or avoid situations. As the fish goes through life, it develops an extensive inventory of sounds that allow it to act, or react well in advance of seeing the sound source."

I started to chuckle. "So what's so goddam funny, Ed?" he quizzed. "Mike," I snorted, "I was picturing those poor fish when you had that fart attack. To those fish it must have sounded like a volcano. The poor buggers are probably still swimming for cover!" It was hard to contain myself. "Man, you can be a real asshole sometimes, Ed... just shut up and listen. Here's some good stuff now."

"The fish has another sensory organ that is able to deal with a different aspect of sound, mainly vibrations. The lateral line is a line of sensory nerve endings on either side of the fish, which complements the hearing from the ears. Among other capabilities, the lateral line can very accurately pick up low frequency vibrations, particularly at a close range of less than 35 feet. Through this apparatus, the fish picks up sounds, which it can learn to distinguish and store in memory. Any sudden sounds that are detected as foreign will make them flee. Yet another capability of the lateral line is its directional honing ability. This can allow the fish to accurately calculate the location of the vibration within 35 feet. Typically a fish will use its ears and the lateral line in combination quite effectively to seek out food types or to avoid danger. This process has evolved as a highly successful survival mechanism in that they are able to distinguish, and locate many different vibrations such as those set off during distress actions. This includes the types of rhythms set up by the swimming action of many different creatures, including their own species."

I had to ask, "Well, so what? What bloody tune are you supposed to play these fish? I may be a dummy but surely if this is true, a fish is sensitive to a particular vibration?"

"Ed, you're not seeing the picture here. Think about all those things you drag in the water that are unfamiliar to the fish. The fish will be attracted by a familiar vibration. It will first hear it and then it will pick it up through the vibrations in the lateral line to target in on the location. This is why the vibrations set up by buzz bombs, spoons or flatfish are effective. They set up interesting vibrations that attract attention. Once they are attracted by the sound, they will locate it by the vibrations. That will get them close enough to see it and strike at it. Think about all the other sounds you make above water that are amplified sounds to the fish. You may understand how easy it is to scare them away. A simple thump on the bottom of the boat will carry amplified sounds through the water that will sound like an explosion to fish. And anyway, this science is what this vibrating lure is all about. Don't you think these guys figured out what vibration was effective? Shit, we are going to empty this lake of fish!"

Well what could I say after that? There was no way I could better that story. If it worked I would never live this one down. On the other hand perhaps I could learn something. "OK, hand me some of that hot gear," I said humbly, "let me take a crack at it." After about 10 minutes and no action Mike told me to come up closer to surface. Half an hour later, no action. "What do you say now Mr. Science?" I taunted, "See those guys over there? They've hauled in two beauties in the last 15 minutes. Maybe their buzzer is vibrating at 300 cycles per minute, or maybe they are humming to those big trout. What do you think about humming a few limericks in b-flat? Maybe you should check that bible of yours and see what frequency makes a fish horny, ha ha…" Mike just leered at me with a scornful eye.

It was an hour later. "I can't stand this horse-shit Mike, those guys are still hauling in fish. I'm going back to my own lure." You could see Mike was a bit irritable now since all that science wasn't too productive. I hauled in and snapped on a fly. "I'll drag this around a while, you can keep vibrating and stimulating their vision."

Just then the other boat trolled by. "How are you guys doing?" I yelled, "I see you hauled out some beauties." The short fat guy stood up beaming and lifted a string of absolutely enormous rainbows. There was one there that had to be two feet long. "Holly shit," Mike squeaked sheepishly, "those are bloody nice fish, what are you using?"

"You know," the short guy said, "it's the dammdest thing... these fish will take anything. It doesn't matter what we drag behind the boat, they just take it. We've used plugs, flies, spinners... man these fish must be hungry. We've got our limits for two days in the last few hours... you guys have been in the same area an hour longer than us, what's your biggest fish?"

God, I thought to myself, *I am sure glad I never treat fishing as a serious matter*.

SOMETIMES HE WAS RIGHT...
BUT NOT OFTEN

The lake was absolutely still. It was now 10:00 AM and the fish were rising everywhere. We figured that we would get out at about the same time as yesterday when they had started to rise. Suddenly I could feel the rhythm of the plug cease, followed by a faint nibble. Almost instinctually I pulled up sharply and started to reel in. There was nothing. Ten pulls out and I sat down in an attempt to regain my composure. "Dammit, that's the third one that's done that to me... I better reel in and sharpen the hooks on that plug. This time I am not pulling, I will set the tension looser and let him go." Mike sat quietly, just watching. After reeling in and carefully sharpening the hooks, I set the tension loose so I could pull it out with two fingers easily. After 40 pulls and 5 minutes I sat back with my feet up pondering those visions of giant trout dragging us across the lake. This time I was not going to be foiled. Wheeeeezzz went Mike's line as it screamed out of the reel. I watched with envy as the fish exploded through the surface. Now it was my turn, I could feel something nibbling. The jerk was almost instinctual, as I jumped up, dropping my beer. But there was no action... nothing pulled anymore... he was gone.

At this point Mike looked out from under his stupid looking hat and began to snort. "I can't stand this any longer, why don't you just sit down and watch the expert for a while. First you want to yank the hook out of his mouth before he has a chance to put it in his mouth, then when you finally let him sample it, you yank it out again. Ed, that's pretty funny considering you are always giving me static about this technical stuff. Man, this is just basics, you've got to let him set the hook, they have a dual sensory system."

"Where do you get this stuff Mike...the hook setter's almanac?"

"Let me just get my line out and I will let you in on a secret. Fish typically have a dual system of taste to add to their arsenal of survival devices. They have the ability to taste through their mouth and through external sensors. There is really little difference between your own ability to see and reject, smell and reject, and even taste and spit out before you swallow. Just imagine what you would do if you put some bad pepperoni in your mouth. They can tell immediately that something is not the real thing and can even discriminate between various tastes such as bitter, sweet, sour or salty tastes just as we can. The sense of taste can be used to determine whether an object such as a lure or plug is recognizable. If a fish has decided to ignore the fact that the object has no smell and take it into its mouth, the lack of taste could still be the trigger that causes it to reject the lure."

He would not stop. "There are many cases where the fish seems to swim by and just nudge the bait with its snout. In such cases, the fish are using the taste sensors placed external to their mouths, located on their lips and snout. These can be so highly developed that they can be used to "pre taste" the food. So if the smell fails, taste at the first level can be the next test. Either ability can give the fish the chance to reject a foreign object before they decide to bite or take it into their mouths. Wouldn't this be a handy ability to have at a seafood buffet? At the next level, the fish can taste the bait when it is in its mouth. At this point the fish can still reject a foreign object even though it is in its mouth. As a matter of fact, the fish can even position the bait in its mouth before it decides to swallow. Needless to say, this sequence of discrimination and rejection can make it difficult to fool a fish long enough to 'set the hook'. If at any point in this process you try to set it by pulling it, you may yank it away from the fish while he is still trying to figure out what this object is, at the first level of sensing. He may have only nudged it with his nose... so don't be too hasty."

It wasn't long before Mike's rod tip started to quiver a bit. "Now the idea is to keep cool, Ed, let him take the hook by himself." The quiver stopped. Just as I was about to start laughing and tell the old goof not to be so smart, the rod tip looked like it was going into spasms. The two-pound beauty broke water about 80 feet behind the boat. Mr. Cool let the tension off a bit, stood up slowly and began a very smug reel-in. "You see, kid, you got to let the hook set."

He was really unbearable the rest of the day. ***Funny things happen to people when they take fishing serious.***

A FRENZY IS WHAT WE REALLY WANT?

Sometimes situations get out of hand. There are those rare occasions where a sequence of events occurs that you could never believe possible. I will never forget the one that had to do with fishing frenzies. We were at a new lake trying our hand at finding that elusive big fish. It was getting to be a bit boring on the water. After 4 hours, the drone of the motor was obscuring the serenity. My beer was finished. If it hadn't been for the wildlife and the peaceful tranquility, I may have been disappointed. After all, we were there to catch those giant rainbows that were lurking in the shadows below us. Mike had changed lures and hung just about every trinket on the line that he had in his box. It seemed that every time I looked up, Mike was mechanically counting pulls. I could sense a frustration in the air. He was starting to look like it was time to be going in for the day. We had stopped the elimination process, and tried just about everything. The two technical wizards of deductive reasoning were beginning to run out of ideas and the stupid fish had outwitted us again.

It was exactly 2:00 PM in the afternoon when I heard a big "plop" over to the left. The sun had disappeared behind the clouds for about 20 minutes now. "Did you see that?" Mike chirped, "That was a big mother!" Mike was starting to fidget so it was time to start a philosophical discussion.

"You know, Ed, these fish must have a pattern to eating. Surely there are times when these fish have supper, dinner, etc., just like other animals. What do you think? I know that there are no guarantees, but I know that fish will most likely feed at dawn and dusk, so to increase your chances of success, you would logically go out at that time. If you are really keen, you can go out in the morning and maybe catch your limit, but what do you do the rest of the day? The big problem is that most of us mortals like to fish during the daytime. Getting out at 5:00 AM or fishing in the cool dusk has its occasional appeal but let's not push it! Maybe this explains why we don't catch as many fish? We choose our preferred time and not the fish's... sort of like making a big dinner arrangement at 10:00 AM?"

It was my turn to start a speech. "Well I've got to believe that just like we anglers like to feed in a cyclic fashion, fish also like to feed in a cyclic fashion. We know they feed for limited periods. We know the bastards also like to start biting and feeding in a group action. The trick, however, is to try to figure out when they will decide to dine. It is not just as simple as breakfast at 8, lunch at 12 and dinner at 6 is it? If fish do have their own rhythmic timing, which we, in all our scientific genius, do not yet understand, what is it that triggers it and how's the time determined? We spend a shitload of time out here and it don't take a genius to see that what will work one day will not necessarily work the next day. You will also note that even on two seemingly equal days, the time at which you catch fish can be quite different. This is most evident during periods when they rise to surface. The fact is that there are active and inactive times during the day where fish, like other animals decide to look for food with some degree of aggression. Sometimes they are fierce and sometimes they are not, but they do not seek food all day long any more than we do. Just as we are actively seeking food three times a day, fish must also seek food. They feed and then rest to digest the food. But fish do not wear wristwatches so it is most likely that other more subtle instinctual timing systems are triggered. Yet another predictable observation is that the feeding period is limited, lasting somewhere between a short 20 minutes to a longer 3 hours. Guess it depends on whether they are having a fondue or visiting McDonalds!"

Mike was starting to get into the conversation with both feet now. "It says in my Fishology book that two major factors will force a fish to feed actively in some form of cyclic pattern. First, digestion takes several hours, which is up to 12 hours typically. It is also a chemical process, which is a function of body temperature that becomes the same as water temperature. If the water is cool it can take much longer. As digestion is occurring their may be little reason for fish to pursue more food simply because it hasn't been activated by the hunger trigger. So if a school of fish prefers to laze around in a thermocline, and all eat together, it is quite likely that they will digest at the same rate and be hungry again at about the same time. Secondly, the fish has only so much energy for active feeding. Twenty minutes to two hours seems to be about the limit. Another cyclic characteristic, which forces inactive time, is the need to rejuvenate the energy level if any exertion has taken place to expend energy. Active feeding and swimming will inevitably force the fish into a rest period, which can take many hours, even up to a day, particularly if there have been any exhausting chases. Because water has four times the heat capacity of air, it can absorb heat very fast from the fish so it has to keep quiet to rejuvenate itself."

"That's really cool," I said, "I've also got to believe that fish are highly competitive. Because of their effective sensing abilities, they must be able to hear, smell, or even see other fish feeding. They must be able to realize this at lengthy distances apart. I'll bet a case of beer that this more often than not will result in a chain reaction, which gets more fish feeding because others are doing so. I'll bet my right nut that it can start by a fish jumping to create a 'splat' on the water, and then it accelerates into a frenzy. This aspect creates the end effect of group feeding frenzies. Either they feel they will miss some choice goodies or they detect an opportunity, but regardless, they can begin to feed quickly and actively."

You could tell that we had started to figure it all out by now. "You know, that's true," said Mike seriously, "I'll bet another factor that adds fuel to this group frenzy idea is that fish also have some social tendencies and tend to school together for social reasons. If they feel better protected or they feel there are more chances of finding food, or there are reproductive reasons, then they are usually hanging around together. When you consider this social action of schooling, it is not that surprising to understand why they may all start feeding together. If they have a tendency to attach themselves to a site, particularly one that has food and shelter, then this also helps to reinforce the groupie feed theory."

The science was getting deeper now. It was like a booze frenzy when a bunch of drunks are closing in on a solution. "Ed, here's some more good stuff in that book of mine that gives some clues. It says that another aspect that can affect metabolism directly is the water and air temperature. As the external air cools and winds blow, they can shift water temperatures, thereby affecting the fish level of activity. These, and night and day variations have direct effects on when fish will feed. Tides are another factor that impact feeding times. The other habits of smaller fish, insects, larvae, or other morsels that they feed on may also behave according to their own rhythms. Their increase in activity can then trigger feeding activities in trout. What is also important is to realize that we are dealing with a species of animal that lives by genetically inherited sophisticated instincts that we do not completely understand. In many situations, these instincts seem to be triggered by something that makes fish feed in mass, during preferred periods, and in an aggressive fashion..."

It was getting pretty heavy now. There were empty beer cans all over the boat and even though the drone of the motor was loud, the splat could be heard loud and clear as the trout's belly flopped on the water. Suddenly we were all very silent... the ripples could be seen radiating out from the epicentre... it was a whale! Then, just 10 seconds later, as we stared at the ripples, a second flash of silver could be seen leaving the water, about 100 feet behind the boat. Mike leapt up as if a hornet had stung him. His beer fell over and crashed to the floor. The rod tip went into spasms as the fish realized it was hooked. And then it took off like a bullet... Mike's reel sounded like a siren.... wheeeeezzz. "Holy sheeeit... look at it go!" Mike gasped, "I've never seen fish strike like that!" Just as Mike began to take up some line I felt a familiar tug. The rod tip gave a few little jerks, then I felt an incredible pull. "Dammit, I must be snagged, what a rotten time for this to happen...no, its loose again...wow! There it is!" A three pounder broke surface... what a sight! Now you could see fish rising everywhere. The lake looked like it was being pelted with cannon balls from the sky. Just then my line started to scream as it tried desperately to get out of the reel.

It was just fantastic; you couldn't get your line out fast enough before another beauty broke the water. Netting was crazy. If anyone would have had a chance to film this netting activity, they would have laughed for weeks... it was as much of a frenzy as the fish feeding. All we could do was throw the fish into the bucket and get the line out. We fished in a frenzy, not even bothering to sharpen hooks and count the pulls. These all became a tedious interference to the excitement.

It was precisely 3:25 PM when everything stopped. No plops, no nibbles, nothing... they had obviously had enough and it was time to rest. We looked at each other in awe. Dead silence. The water was as flat as glass. The boat was a mess. I was at the motor. We survived the tornado.

"Holy shit," Mike yelped, "was that not something? How many did we catch?" He brought the bucket up on the seat to have a look. It was at that moment that a strange sequence unravelled itself. Mike's beer can was on the edge of the boat.

A mosquito bit him fiercely on the neck. He turned to swat it and knocked the beer can over the side. Bending over to reach it, his rod fell victim to a massive tug. Turning swiftly to more important actions, his nice new hat flopped into the water. "Fuck", he yelled, "get my new hat, I've got a monster on here!" The once slack line had, however, gone beneath the motor so when he yanked the rod up, the rod broke. A massive fish exploded out of the water. I had stopped the motor to reach his hat. As I reached out I got my own tug. "I can't," I yelled, "you're on your own!"

Mike stood up in the scrawny boat in an attempt to grab the other chunk of the rod. As he leaned over, he lost his balance and crashed towards the middle seat. Before he hit, the boat leaned sideways, he knocked the bucket off the seat where he had placed it to count the fish. How that bucket decided to fall out of the boat is a mystery but out it went. Now there were two monsters on the lines. The boat now stopped had turned sideways, with the two fish rocketing out of the water on the same side. Mike smashed into the open lure box and everything came out onto the floor. As his belly hit the seat, his head hit the cooler and his glasses went sailing over the side. The cooler tipped over and the contents, mostly loose ice, water, beer and pepperoni exploded onto the floor. With his one arm still up in the air holding his precious half rod, Mike was still determined to get that fish. Now it was my turn. I had leaned sideways and the boat was pitched at about 45 degrees. I lurched the other way in an attempt to stabilize the boat. The net, leaning against the side flopped into the water. I lost the grip on my rod; over the side and off it went as the monster decided to take its last run at that precise moment. The motor that was not quite in its socket, had come off the transom at the last tilt. I could see it falling and lurched to grab it. I just got hold of the gas line as it hit the water. Now I was spread-eagled over the transom holding onto the motor. "Mike," I screamed, "where the fuck are you? I need some help on this motor!" Mike was bent over the seat trying to get up, still holding the bro-

150

ken rod in his hand. As he clambered to my end of the boat, my end of the boat quickly dropped. "Get back or you'll sink us," I bellered before my face hit the water.

Somehow, I got the motor back as Mike lurched backwards to try to stabilize the boat. How the line held the motor I don't know but it was as bizarre as the events that seemed to just keep rolling. I got the motor back on and finally looked forward.

I couldn't believe it. Mike was there reeling on his broken rod, still after that fish. To his dismay, however, there was one more burst out of the water, the fish threw the hook and disappeared.

All we could do is look at each other in disbelief. Only a minute had elapsed. We had lost all the fish, hat, rod, glasses, and net in that short time. The boat looked like a tornado hit it. No one would ever believe how this happened. There were two beer on the floor. I leaned over and grabbed them, tossing one to him. "Have a beer, Mike", I said, "I guess we also know what a frenzy is! And we still don't know when those bloody fish eat meals!"

There was dead silence for about 10 seconds. The laughter that ensued could be heard for miles around I am sure. *Yes, I thought to myself, how could anybody ever get serious about fishing?*

THE FRENZY REVISITED

As we sat around the table in the cabin, we recalled the fishing frenzy of the day. "Man that was something else," said Mike, "but we still haven't figured out why they started to bite at that time. We were there at the same time yesterday and there wasn't even a nibble. I read that you always increase the odds of catching fish in the early morning or late evening, the times when the sun rises and sets. All the experts swear that the first two hours after daybreak and the last two hours before dark are likely active surface feeding times for fish. I know you think this is all horseshit Ed, but my book reinforces this. It says that there are seven reasons why a fish should feed closer to surface at dawn. It takes 12 hours to digest food, they wake up hungry after a night's rest and their day vision is ready to go at daybreak. In addition, the water is cooler at surface where the surface water can mix with oxygen. Finally, they are well rested with energy levels high plus other creatures, including food are active. Under such conditions, all you need is someone to start feeding and trigger a feeding frenzy. Doesn't this reinforce our frenzy idea?"

"Mike, this is all well and good, but I am not so keen to wake up at the crack of dawn. It's a bit of a challenge even for you. The evening may be a bit better. I guess you could only hypothesize that as dark approaches, the feeding habits could be stimulated in preparation for the long fast through the night. Sort of like us eating dinner at sundown. Evening feeding can be equally active, but not quite as predictably active. If all your physiology stuff is right then the fish adjust their vision to acute night vision and the light intensity has decreased by that time. The evening has cooled the surface waters, and other life such as insect life is active so the fish needs supper before bedtime."

"OK, let's try the morning out for the first time, Ed. I know it's difficult to get up early but let's check out the breakfast frenzy. The locals have given us many clues on what to use and where to try. The best is a Muddler fly made out of deer hair, one of the local camp experts told us, but you can draw them out with Spratleys and Mosquitoes. Over there where the stream enters the lake is a long deep channel, they seem to hang about in that area most of the time. They said there are 6-pound trout in that hole. We know where and what to use, let's check out when. Wouldn't a 5-pounder get your ass out there at 4:00 AM?"

"Four AM! Come on Mike…" I whimpered, "that's heavy, but I agree. I will do it this once." That was all he needed to hear … it was a long time since we caught anything that big! It was time to take a more serious attack at these monsters… but this time it was time to break tradition and even test some science. We were going to try fishing at dawn! This would be a pretty difficult experience for us… the girls would no doubt refuse to even con-sider getting out of the sack at 4:00 AM! But if we could catch one 6-pound fish it would be worth it.

The evening was stormy. A thunderstorm moved in from the north and the rain was in-tense. It was a fantastic evening, listening to the rain pelting the shake roof. We were all out like a light at 10:00 PM, after our tackle and plans were put in place. The storm con-tinued throughout the night. Morning came fast, 3:30 is an awful time for a mortal to rise on a vacation, but we were on the water, heading for that deep channel at 4:00 AM. It was still quite dark and it was actually hard to believe that we were out here. Fortunately, the storm had stopped just before we left the dock - a good piece of luck! The sky was now clearing and the wind stopped. The lake was losing its chop. And just over the landscape you could see the light glowing faintly over the horizon as the dawn started to break. We had actually forgotten how fantastic this could be. At 4:20 we were cruising over the channel, Mike with a Tom Thumb just below surface and I dragging a Blue Flatfish. You could see signs of fish rolling and surfacing. Maybe these fish had dropped to the bottom for 12 hours and missed a meal because of the storm. Could we be lucky enough to encounter some ravenous trout?

"Ed this has to be a perfect scene... its a classic text book situation, why haven't we had a strike yet? Pass me the thermos." Just as Mike reached over to take the thermos, his rod end jerked and the rod snapped against the floor. He grabbed for it in shear panic. Mike had set the tension tight expecting a whale to bite. Now that the whale was on the line, it was about to pull his rod out of the boat! What a sight, the thermos crashed to the floor just as the fish broke water. It was an incredible sight in the low light. Then my rod tip started its dance.

It took Mike a few minutes to haul in that trout. It was exactly eight inches long. I lost mine. "Mike," I said, "are you really going to keep that minnow, I'd be embarrassed to take it back?" "Piss off Ed, at least I got one!" was the response. For the next two hours we sat there looking at each other shivering in the cool air. No nibbles, no risers, no nothing. By sunrise we were a couple of unhappy lads. "Fuck this," said Mike, "I've had enough, I give up. Let's head in for breakfast." There was no way I was going to argue.

We were 100 yards from the dock, just starting to haul the lines in when we both felt the tug of a whale at the end of our lines*. **I knew right then that there was no way that anybody should take fishing serious**.

WHEN YOU'RE HOT
YOU'RE HOT?

The evening was upon us and we had settled into the cabin, time to recall the fishing highlights of the day. Unfortunately, there were few fish caught except for some small ones. As the evening advanced, the conversation became more and more philosophical. We started to talk about when was the best time to fish. There were many times that we hit fish feeding frenzies but how could one time this? I started the discussion.

"I've noticed that there are always times when you seem to depend on luck to hit a feeding time. We all know that there are times when the fish feed in a frenzy and other times when they are less fierce. They will ignore feed on one day and strike hard on others. And when it starts, it typically lasts for about two hours. Sometimes when the frenzy hits, they will take almost anything you drag in front of them. The fact of the matter is that we have both seen these preferred periods of time during the day when fish feed in greater numbers and with greater aggression. Surely there must be some logical reason for this?"

Mike was quick to interrupt. "You know, all the experts who fish on the ocean like to use tide tables. Why? Because tide tables are a readily acceptable aid that helps identify specific times of the day to fish. Nobody gets excited or calls you an idiot when you tell them that tide tables have been produced as a result of knowing the position of the moon through the year. In simplistic terms, the magnetic pull of the moon will have the end result of 'pulling' the water away from the land, known as 'ebb' or towards the land, known as 'flood', depending on where it is and how close it is to the earth. The intensity of this will of course vary, causing the difference in the high to low tides, as will the time difference as the moon changes positions. This is hardly rocket science so why should the variation in water height be unique to the ocean. The same sort of action occurs on other bodies of water, probably not to the same degree, simply because of the smaller volume of water. To a salt water angler, the tide tables and the times shown represent key periods when certain things happen that can stimulate feeding in fish. Thus the correlation with tide times is indirect rather than direct. So why not apply this to the trout in a lake?"

"Mike you're absolutely right," I cut in, "when you really think about it, they pay attention to slack water and the two hours surrounding slack water when tides change. When the incoming tide meets the outgoing, the two flows come together to create a time of 'slack water'. This time, which is not normally any longer than a few hours, gives fish a chance to move around without battling currents, and to chase other fish that also may become active. Where the two opposite currents meet, a 'tide line' is formed as a line of froth and junk that marks the join of waters as they meet. This is marked by foam, debris, attracting feeding birds, and various other life forms to create a gathering place for food for all marine life. As the tide comes out from the land, it carries debris and foodstuff that will attract this activity, and this will also attract feeding fish. Slack water will occur for about a two-hour period around high tide and around low tide. Both these times should be considered as possible heightened fishing activities."

"I think that water flow is also a key item." said Mike, "The tide tables, and the difference in height can give you an indication of the degree of current and its direction. If the water flows past a point of land, in a southerly direction, then back eddies will form on the downside. If a specific fishing hole is known to be good, then you can predict the best time of circulating water that will interest the fish (bringing in food) and at the same time offer areas of protection from harsh currents. The water flow, regardless of intensity, will have a tendency to disturb and move small organisms, particularly algae. Such action will activate the food chain participants to feed. Quite often, feeding occurs when an area becomes flooded by a high tide, allowing fish to come into areas not readily accessible at other times. This creates feeding opportunities that can trigger things, and is quite easily predicted as the high tide time."

"I think that these all serve in helping the fish 'decide' when to start setting out the cutlery. The tide tables just allow you to predict ahead of time when this could be. I've got to believe the same tidal effect takes place on lakes, just simply reduced substantially so that it is not noticeable. The fact is that the moon pulls lake waters just as easily as the ocean waters. The effects are much more subtle, but nevertheless, they are still there. The overall effect of this is not noticeable on a small lake because the body of water is not large enough to be effected by a direct gravitational pull. It is much more pronounced on large lakes where you will actually get a rise and fall of the lake level. Nevertheless, regardless of size, the tidal pull is still there."

"Goddamit, that's smart Mike," I encouraged him, "the other consideration in all this is that we seldom fish the same waters consistently enough to determine any patterns, so we have a tendency to disbelieve any correlation with lunar mechanisms, but there is no doubt that the sun and the moon play key roles in influencing feeding habits. Most experts will verify that the sun and moon are causing situations that get the fish active. This is the 'causal' approach, suggesting that the moon causes it indirectly; it does not 'trigger' the fish to act directly. Such a suggestion could prove to be a bit off base, weird, and even goofy! But whether we believe it or not, these two celestial bodies may influence behaviour more that we like to admit. And just because our scientists can't provide definitive proof that the moon triggers certain activities, this does not mean that it isn't so. After all, do we know all the laws of behaviour? Hardly!"

Now things were really getting hot. By now there was a table full of empty beer cans. Mike got a new brain wave. "Lets go a step further. Let us not forget the human desire to eat three meals a day according to the cycles of the sun. Let's not forget the fact that we sleep when the sun sinks and wake when it rises. Is this because it gets dark? I don't think so. The big question is how do you get tide tables for the lakes... Well I think I've got the answer. Ever heard of Solunar Tables?"

Not really," I said, "are they those little books like tide tables I've seen at the fishing stores?"

"Your are absolutely right, little brother," exclaimed Mike, "let me teach you some really cool science. A solunar period is a word coined to reflect solar and lunar odd hour periods when heightened activities can be predicted in various wildlife. The lunar day is 24 just a bit under 25 hours, within which four odd hour periods occur. Solunar combines the Solar and Lunar cycles. The suggestion is that sun up and sun down cycle has a dramatic effect on fish feeding, and may even predict the intensity. Consider the moon up and moon down as another possibility. Just because you can't see it doesn't mean it isn't happening. The moon has its own up and down just like the sun, as well as its own intensity. This is most obvious when the full moon rises over the horizon. Remember that fish are quite capable of seeing in the moonlight, so to a fish, moon up could be just as good as sun up! Well these cycles are quite predictable in advance, and the various up and down cycles of the sun and moon are detailed in a set of tables, called solunar tables, that can be purchased, much like tide tables."

"No shit," I said as I reached for an ale, "this is going to change our habits. This all makes sense, but there must be some hitches. I got to believe that these 'hot times' can be disturbed by changes in weather, barometric levels, temperature, so the idea is that this is not an absolute method, it only identifies the most likely time when fish will feed, right? If you want to increase your chances of hitting a feeding time then this is the way to do it. Our primary thesis is that birds, game, animals, and perhaps even humans become more active during these periods. So let's not make this an absolute set of rules so we don't get laughed at. We just say that we feel that from experience that to really enhance your chances of hitting a fish feeding frenzy, choose a solunar period."

"Well, we've got to test this stuff," said Mike. The beer and the excitement were getting to be too much. It was time to carry the excitement into the next day.

Much to our surprise, when we sheepishly asked the people at the lodge about solunar tables we got quite a surprise. "No, we ran out last week," the proprietor said, "but if you have a set of coastal tide tables I can tell you how to use them instead." Mike and I looked at each other with the thought that our new discovery was actually old hat. What a horrible thought. Why didn't we know about this? Mike was quick to respond without looking too stupid. "Yes I have a set in the truck."

"Well, those tables which give you the high and low tides actually correlate with the minor and major feeding times in the solunar tables. All you have to do is follow the path of the moon and calculate when that same pull on the coast will occur inland on the lake you're at. Pretty simple hey? Here all you do is add about 30 minutes for each 250 miles of eastward traverse."

We had planned to fish at a major period which we calculated as starting at 2:00 PM. Mike had pulled the Vancouver tide tables out of the truck. The tide tables indicated that in Vancouver, the low tide was at 12:30 PM. Adding an hour for daylight saving time made this 1:30 PM. Looking at the map, we were about 250 miles inland from the coast so we added 30 minutes as about the time that a low tide equivalent would be at the lake. We figured to add about 30 minutes for every 250 miles eastward and that's about how far inland we were. But to adjust for errors due to Mike's astronomical 'expertise', we decided that we would need to get out well before this time and fish through the 'hot period'. The weather had been unsettled and stormy, dumping rain sporadically. In fact, we were out there by 11:00 AM. The wind had picked up stirring up the water, continuing to create a steady chop that made trolling difficult. We fished the 'hot period' faithfully, with little success. The storm had probably sent them deeper. The fishing was dismal, except for the odd small one that we had to throw back. The only salvation was that no one else had much of a good day either. This we found out when we came in late in the afternoon.

It was time to plan out the next day's strategy. "Tomorrow the major hot time would be at about 2:30 PM Ed, I have a better feeling for us limiting out. The weather is supposed to settle down as well. We should fish a few hours in the morning but let's go out with our whole arsenal at 1:30 PM. The area where the creek cuts a channel into the lake will be hot for sure. That's where we got the nibbles today."

The next morning was indeed glorious. It was a treat to meet it. Our morning fish was mediocre, hauling in just enough for our late breakfast. But the afternoon session was much different. We knew the most likely feeding depth, and the most likely bait, so we had a head start. We did get out there at 1:30 PM but there was no action. It was about 2:20 when things started to happen, just out of nowhere. We had actually settled back to enjoy the scenery and the tranquility of it all when it started.

The first thing that happened was that Mike's line came across and tangled with mine. I was trolling a small spinner so Mike took a sweep with the boat. His line crossed and the ends tangled. As the line started its irregular movements, it was rather obvious that we had a problem. But at that moment Mike's rod also got a huge tug. He was almost instinctual in reeling in. "Hey, what about the tangle?" I bellered, "We've got to haul in and untangle." "No way, man, I've got a bruiser on, so just reel yours in slow, along with mine so I don't loose this fish."

As he reeled in, the fish broke surface, displaying its silver side and disappeared heading deep. "Wow, feel that baby go!" Mike screeched as the fish picked up energy and the rod tip took the strain, "I've got to let him run, better give him some running room and release the tension a bit." Mike reached down to twist the tension knob on the front of his spinning reel and his shirt cuff caught the line guide, flipping it open. Well that fish took off like a shot since the line could now go freely off the reel. "Shit," Mike screamed, as he fumbled to flip it back. But it was an impossible task as that line was singing out at a hell of a speed so he grabbed the line with his fingers to slow it. Realizing that wasn't going to work he let it go but the line continued to shoot out from the momentum causing an instant bird's nest to gather and catch at the top guide. With the line at least stopped, Mike's next brilliant move was to start reeling in but the nest got would around the reel as it came closer.

Now Mike could release or reel in. "Goddammit! That's the biggest fuckin fish I've had, there's no way that sonofabitch is getting away." Mike then dropped his rod, reached for the line at the end and started to pull in a few feet at a time, dropping the gathers at his feet. Somehow that fish was still on. I gave up reeling in because the comedy that was developing at the other end of the boat was pretty hard to ignore. That rainbow torpedoed out of the water, dove and headed down again, right under the boat. "Jeezuz, Ed, don't sit there like a dumb turd, do something... can't you net the bastard yet? There he is... get him..." As the fish disappeared, Mike turned sideways to see where the fish went and missed his overhand stroke on pulling the line. The huge loops at his feet, which now tangled around Mike's Fly fishing rod, immediately started to shoot out in a huge bird's nest, with the rod in it. Mike now lunged to save his rod. It was too much for me to watch and I started to laugh. Mike got mad but there was little he could do. Now on the other side of the boat, the fish, a massive ten-pound rainbow, took one last leap out of the water, had a look at the comedy, spit the hook and was gone.

Mike just looked dazed. Silently he started to haul the line into the boat. Luckily, the line had tangled around the reel so in came the rod as he pulled. After another 30 feet, in came my line, tangled and twisted around Mike's. The tangle and mess in the boat was something to see. Fish were surfacing everywhere. I guess the big brute went down to tell all his buddies about the fiasco and it was time for a group laugh. There we were, sitting in a tangle of lines, lures and rods. It was at least 40 minutes before we got it all straightened out and re-rigged. Mike just didn't seem to have his usual sense of humour.

Finally, we got our lines back into the water. We were about 10 minutes into it, when Mike finally said: "Ed, have you noticed the smart bastards have stopped rising... the feeding frenzy is over." We looked at each other and started to laugh. There was only one thing to do. In unison, the next words came out simultaneously: ***Fuckit, we're taking this too serious, let's have a beer!***

MORE HUMOUR BY Ed Rychkun

Corporations Stripped Naked: Exposing the AQ Virus

Want a fresh, new humorous look at the business world

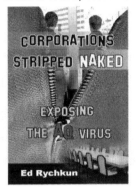

we all live in? Take a tour of corporate life through former business executive Ed Rychkun's view of his lifetime of climbing corporate ladders. This provocative and hilarious expose' shows what really goes on behind those boardroom walls. It reveals the flip side of a company's naked underbelly by showing how people universally conform to laws on how they feel about each other called AQ'ISM – a classification of "Asshole".

Ed examines the social behavior of corporate citizens and develops his universal laws about how this feeling is quantified as an AQ, and how it can have a direct impact on how fast you can climb or fall from the corporate ladder. Ed tells it like it is, revealing how the "real" professionals - the Executives, use a set of secret AQ Arsenals to hide their incompetence and maintain their positions of power in the corporate hierarchy by making asses of others. You will immediately recognize a similarity with your own situation and derive humor from it. But beware, as one critic points out, *"Never was the raw naked truth so aptly expressed as in this earthy examination of the blatantly exposed underbelly of the modern corporation".*

Corporations Stripped Naked: Controlling the AQ Virus

In this sequel to ***Corporations Stripped Naked: Exposing the AQ Virus***, Author and former business executive Ed Rychkun takes you deeper into the naked corporations secret tactical AQ arsenals. He strips companies naked of their professionalism and glamour to bare the Executive and Management tools of power and control that gravitate into a darker side of the AQ virus and a universal phenomenon he dubs the AQ. Using his own 30 years of climbing ladder to the top, he exposes how top management falls victim to a viral cross between the Peter Principle and the IQ. Using large Fortune 500 companies, as well as smaller enterprises as his stage, Ed relates his first hand experience in maintaining positions of Managers, VP, CEO, Founder, Director, and Chairman. Find out what really takes place behind closed boardroom doors. Get a new perspective on a naked corporation as Ed reveals what the real experts, the Executives and the Managers, use as universal tactics and tricks called the AQ Arsenals to hide their incompetence and climb the corporate ladders fast; and to maintain order and control. See how you can monitor your progress and avoid the AQ Virus of moving to the dark side of corporate life.

www.edrychkun.com